Wanting a God
You Can Talk To

Wanting a God You Can Talk To

by Jesse Duplantis

20 19 18 17   8 7 6 5 4 3 2

2nd printing, December 2017

Wanting a God You Can Talk To
ISBN: 978-160683-492-3
Copyright © 2001 by Jesse Duplantis

Published in Partnership
Jesse Duplantis Ministries
P.O. Box 1089
Destrehan, Louisiana 70047
www.jdm.org

Harrison House Publishers
Tulsa, OK 74145
www.harrisonhouse.com

Jesse Duplantis Ministries is dedicated to reaching people and changing lives with the Gospel of Jesus Christ. For more information or to purchase other products from Jesse Duplantis Ministries, please contact us at the address above.

Dedication

This book is dedicated to all those who have walked up to me after a church service and said, "Brother Jesse, I wish God would talk to me the way He talks to you!" I wrote this book with you in mind! I hope my book helps you to recognize God's voice more clearly so you can enjoy the wonderful and intimate relationship with God that you desire.

Table of Contents

CHAPTER 1

The God of
My Childhood

All I ever wanted was a God I could talk to. But when I was growing up, God wasn't somebody you had a conversation with. I am a Cajun French boy, who grew up along the bayous of South Louisiana and the banks of the Mississippi River. My dad worked in the oil industry, and our family moved around South Louisiana quite a-lot. Every move meant we were going to a new church, and I experienced many different denominations in my childhood. When kids at a new school would ask me, "What religion are you?" I'd say, "Pick one. I've been there."

If you grew up in South Louisiana, you had to be Catholic at least once. I was christened a Catholic boy. Ninety-nine percent of the people I knew were Catholic too, because they were the only ones that would come to our area and talk about God! You've got to give it to the Catholics. They had a plan! A lot of people criticize the Catholic church, but I don't because they went out and they did something for the world—converting people and building churches every step of the-way.

So as a young Catholic boy in the nineteen fifties, the church *was God* to me. I didn't even think of God in terms of having a personality. To me, wherever the church was, that's where God was, and I left God sitting in the pew when I walked out of the church doors after mass.

In those days, nobody talked to God. If you wanted to and had the guts to say so, people would look at you like you were arrogant. They'd say something like, "Who do you think you are, boy? You can't talk to God! Go talk to the priest!"

God was not available. So you left a message with His servant and didn't expect to be called back anytime soon. If you did feel like you were worthy enough to talk straight to God, you were still taught that it was a one-way conversation. Nobody ever told you that God would talk back. And if you were hearing anybody talking back to you when you prayed, you were crazy and just didn't know it!

We Have a Connection to Heaven

Then something wild happened in our family. Dad got "saved" and we switched from the Catholic church to the Baptist church. Talk about culture shock. I'll never forget when my parents asked me, "Jesse, do you want to get saved?"

"From what?"

They had to explain it to me. Back then Catholics didn't use terms like "saved" and "born again." Those were Baptist words. In fact, I learned a whole new language in the Baptist church. Words like "training union" and "vacation Bible school" became part of my Cajun vocabulary. No more Catechism for me—it was Sunday school, training union, and vacation Bible school. In other words, school, school, and more school. And the services were longer too.

Now, in the Baptist church I attended, all the sermons and Sunday school lessons centered on the big "don'ts." Because after you got "saved," that's what you concentrated on. The top three don'ts were: Don't smoke, don't drink, and don't run around with women.

They did preach that you could talk to God and criticized the Catholics for sending you to talk to the saints and the priest. But you were never supposed to expect God to actually talk back to you. Now, at least we were encouraged to pray often to God and we were always told He would forgive us no matter what. But nobody was told to expect much from God in the way of conversation. You were supposed to be happy and grateful for your salvation, simply hope God heard you when you prayed, and go on living a decent life.

So talking to God and asking Him for things was still a gamble because, as they said and I heard this so much in Southern Louisiana that I can repeat it exactly like they said it, "You know how God is. Sometimes He does and sometimes He don't." We heard that so much, it should have been printed on a plaque outside the church doors right after John 3:16! Like a gospel casino, you figured you had a fifty-fifty shot at God actually hearing you. He was a busy God, and you just hoped and wished you'd get lucky and get Him to hear you and answer your prayer.

I'm not being critical of all Baptists, of course, because I love the Baptist denomination, and I really believe that they have a greater understanding of grace and redemption than almost any other denomination. My life was completely changed because of a Baptist minister who told me about a merciful Jesus! So I have nothing against them at all, and I'm grateful for their amazing contribution to Christianity. But as a kid going to the church our family went to, Jesus wasn't really accessible. I was just never taught that God would actually talk back to me. Maybe He'd talk to the preacher, but not me.

So, when I was asked, "Would you like to be born again?" I thought, *I was lucky I was born once.* I had no real understanding of the concept of spiritual rebirth, because I didn't understand how anybody could have a "personal relationship with Jesus."

If you didn't expect Him to talk back to you, how could you ever get to know Him? That was my young mind's reasoning. When I was asked, "Would you like to make a public profession of your faith?" I said, "I don't have any." And I was right.

I didn't have any real faith, so I sure didn't need to make a public profession! I went to church with my parents and heard all the "be good, be nice" lessons; but I felt God was distant, up in the sky, and busy taking care of other people's business. Why should I work hard at being good and nice if He didn't care about me?

We went to that church for a while, but then something else happened to my dad, and it sent shock waves through our family. By accident, Dad got something he called the Holy Ghost! He started to speak in a language the church people called tongues.

So the Baptists kicked us out of the church. They thought that speaking in tongues was something straight from the devil, and they didn't want the devil in their church. So out we went! For me, that meant there would be no more training union and vacation Bible school. No more hour and a half services either.

When we moved over to the Pentecostal church, Sunday services became an all-day event. During the week, you could go to church almost every night too! Revival could last for six weeks! I thought, *Man, Catholic mass is thirty minutes. Baptist church services are about an hour. But at this church, we're never getting out!*

The truth was that Daddy had enough trouble with the English language. He was Cajun French, and sometimes his French blended with his English. Now he had a prayer language to add to the mix and it sounded like African Zulu. I'd listen to Dad pray and I'd think, *He's been watching those movies about Africa again!*

When Dad asked me, "Would you like to get the Holy Ghost, son?" I didn't want it. It sounded weird, and besides, everybody down at the Pentecostal church seemed weird.

As a kid, I thought the Pentecostals were the loudest people I'd ever seen in church. I couldn't believe my eyes when I'd watch them practically running to the altar screaming, bawling and squawling, "Ohhhhhhhhhhh Gawd! Gawd! Gawd! Help me, Gawd! Help me!"

I thought, *God help these people!* There was some serious business going on at the altar every service. People would shake and cry all day long if you let them. They really didn't so much as talk or pray to God; it's more like they screamed at Him! They hollered at Him! They'd even raise their hands up to the church ceiling just to get closer to Him. I thought it was the weirdest thing I'd ever seen, and I'd already seen a lot of weird things by that time in my young life.

These people loved church so much, they were there every time the doors opened. They sang and ran around the church. For us, prayer took on a whole new meaning—nothing happened until you "prayed through," which usually meant prayer went on until after midnight. That's when the action happened and *wham!* After praying and screaming all day, people heard from God in the midnight hour.

I never understood why they just didn't wait until eleven o'clock at night to start praying. If God wasn't going to show up until midnight, what's the point of beating your brains out all afternoon and-night?

I had more culture shock when it came to their Sunday school! Training union was easy in comparison to the Sunday school lessons at this church! I'm not being critical of all Pentecostal churches because I know that not all of them are the same; but at this church, you sat in Sunday school while the teacher fired away the Hell-fire and brimstone sermons at you until the guilt and fear set into your mind really good.

Everything seemed to be a sin at this church. If you liked doing it, chances are it was a sin! And if it wasn't one yet, it would become one just as soon as you said you liked it!

Of course, the top three no-no's from the last church we went to were still a sin: no smoking, no drinking, no running around with women. But here the sin list was a mile long and nobody had it worse than the women. For women, wearing make-up was a sin, cutting their hair was a sin, wearing pants was a sin, and even wearing sleeveless shirts was a sin!

Today I think, *Man, if an armpit turns you on, you need God!* But back then I just looked around and thought, *These are the plainest, most miserable looking women I've ever seen!* These poor women had to wear big, long, flour-sack looking dresses and hair wrapped in buns on top of their heads that were so tight, they lived in a perpetual state of aggravation. Tight buns were not the style back then, believe me, so you could pick out the women from our church from a mile away! And a dot of blush would get the other women in the church fuming and whispering, "Why just look at that Jezebel! Got that make-up on her face, the little Jezebel!"

What I never understood as a kid was why the men in the church even bothered marrying. I mean, if a woman was so bad, why did every man in the church want one? I'd say something like that and get a slap for even thinking it. It was nuts!

Men and boys had to deal with their own sin. If you were a guy and your hair was long enough to cover your ears, it was a sin. It had to be cut really short or you were going to Hell. At that church, even playing sports was a sin.

Now, I loved baseball. I loved the game. I loved the uniform. I loved everything about it, and I was good at it too. I won lots of trophies as a young boy. Dad would drive me to the games, and it was one of the only outlets I had that was legal. When we started going to the Pentecostal church, I quickly learned that my favorite sport was a Hell-fire sin too. I couldn't believe it.

Dad didn't really agree with them, but it wasn't too long before he stopped taking me to the games. It wasn't that Dad really believed that baseball was a sin. He just didn't want to catch flack from the other members of the church. So he told me I could hitchhike if I wanted to go. I did, but I ended up quitting because I couldn't always get there by hitchhiking. If no one picked me up, I'd miss a game or I'd be so late that I was embarrassed.

Here, everything was a sin. The only thing you could do was eat food. And *did* they eat! Man, these people could flat eat some food! The women were so fat that it came up out of their shoes, and the men had giant fifty-pound bellies that hung over their belt buckles.

I suddenly saw the hypocrisy; I'd point it out to my mom and get slapped. I just didn't understand why somebody who came to the church smelling like smoke would be damned to Hell, while these people could wolf down gumbo and stew by the barrel-full and nobody even mentioned the word gluttony.

If smoking is so bad, what's so good about eating until you're obese? I imagined you could throw pizzas at these people like Frisbees and they'd catch them with their mouth and gobble them down whole. But, hey, what else were they going to do since everything else was a sin? The only pleasurable thing left was food! I didn't care whether they were fat or not, I just wanted them to let me play ball and stop harping on the smokers!

At the Pentecostal church we went to, some of the women were flat-out mean. Maybe it was their tight buns. There was this old woman there who was so coarse and mean, I thought she must have shaved her legs with a weed-eater. That was one mean woman! I bet she put gunpowder in her biscuits. This old woman always had this tight frown on her face, was always criticizing somebody for something. She'd sit in church and stare at you like you were the worst kid on earth. Her eyes told you that if she could smack the fire out of you when your mama wasn't looking, she would. Talk about a mean old lady! I, and every other kid I knew in the church, stayed as far away from her as possible.

Now, at the Pentecostal church we went to, God wasn't quite as distant as the other churches we'd gone to. In fact, you were told you could expect an answer when you prayed to God. But, make no mistake, you weren't going to get that answer without a real fight. Serious travail was going to have to happen first, and you could only expect that answer if you were willing to put your time in and be perfect in the process. Prayer was hard and involved long hours of begging, pleading, and bawling at the altar.

Suffering was a major part of the process. They warned you that God was always waiting to throw you in Hell if you messed up. One sin could send you there, but if you asked for forgiveness, you were back on the road to Heaven.

I was in and out of Hell so much as a kid in this church, I didn't know what to do with myself! I never really ever felt good enough. It was always about attaining, attaining, and attaining—never reaching God. And that was just too hard for me.

THE GOD OF MY CHILDHOOD

On top of that, my church preached that Hell was so hot that in Sunday school I was afraid to open my mouth and speak to God because He might be in a bad mood and "smite" me! At that church, I learned the importance of not ticking God off. People would say, "You better not do that, boy. God'll kill you, boy!"

I'd think to myself, *Well, I ain't talking to Him*!

My Dad was so fired up about God and being filled with the Holy Ghost and speaking in tongues that it wasn't long before he was out preaching and witnessing on street corners. He'd taught me to play the guitar at five years old, so I'd stand out there on the corner and play as he preached salvation to the people who walked by.

It was embarrassing to me as a kid to play while people sneered at us on the corner. But it wasn't long before Daddy moved from the street corner to the church. He became a Pentecostal pastor, and that came with its own set of rules for me, like playing music at church. It also meant I had to play music at the church down the road when they needed it. Dad would lend me out to his pastor friend when they didn't have anybody else.

As a kid in this kind of church, I figured that the best thing I could do when it came to dealing with God was to shut up. After all, He was mad and I knew that if I talked to Him, I'd only make Him madder. Whippings from God weren't light. They came as things like broken legs, sudden car accidents, sickness, disease, and a hot Hell of an afterlife.

Do you get my point?

God Was Listening After All

It's kind of funny to me now because I know so much more about God. I now know He is a loving and merciful God Who really wants to have a relationship with His kids. His thoughts may be higher than ours, but He's still willing to talk, and He wants to guide us so we get the most out of His precious gift called life. Today I don't live under the pressure of the distant, angry God of my childhood.

I've grown up.

I've wised up.

I've found the real God and learned a thing or two about His personality. And I've had the incredible opportunity of spending every day since then talking to Him.

And guess what?

He talks back to me.

No, I'm not crazy. And no, I'm not dodging lightning bolts every time I mess up in life and need forgiveness. What I found was a real friend and a true Father. I found a God that I can talk to.

Some people don't believe that I really have a relationship with God, but I don't care what people say or think about me because I know it's true. I'm not out to convince people that God is real and that He can talk to them. I've never read once in the Bible where Jesus tried to convince people He was God's Son. You never hear Him trying to drum it up by saying, "Come on! I am the Son of God! I really am! You've just gotta believe me! I am! I am! I am the Son of God!"

So I follow His example by not trying to beat people over the head with the truth. Truth is truth. Whether people accept truth or not, well, that's up to them. I'm simply writing this book to share my story and to share some of what I've learned about communicating with God, understanding some of what He's written in the Bible, and simply enjoying life as a believer in Jesus Christ.

Joy is my favorite part about knowing God. I love having peace in my life instead of all that turmoil I witnessed as a kid! I've learned that God can go beyond the four walls of the church. I've learned that He's not looking for ways to hurt me. I now know that the "never-good-enough" mentality of my childhood was a falsity.

There is an illusion that most people have about God. They think that religion and God go hand-in-hand. But they don't. Going to church doesn't guarantee you'll know God. I went to church my whole childhood and didn't ever really know God. Do you know why? Because knowing somebody, even if He is the Somebody Who created the universe, is a personal thing.

When I was a kid in church, all I ever wanted was a God I could talk to. While I may not have had a two-way relationship with God back then, I definitely have it today! I found what I was looking for in a bathroom of all places. I guess you could say I met God at the "throne." I'll tell more about that in the next chapter.

I don't want you to get the wrong impression though. By this time in my life, I wasn't exactly looking for God. I'd long given up on religion, and I had no interest in knowing God.

I'd become a rock musician, playing Led Zeppelin, Grand Funk, and Deep Purple style rock-n-roll. I'd been playing music since I was a kid. By the time I was ten years old, I was sneaking out of the house to visit local bars and play my guitar for tips in and around New Orleans.

I'd go to school in the day, work a job from afternoon to nightfall, and sneak out of the house to play music late at night. I did that all through junior high and high school, and during those years, I made more money a year than my dad did. People will pay to be entertained, and music became my ticket out of South Louisiana.

In 1970, I married my wife, Cathy, and got out of Louisiana. By then, I'd already formed the opinion that churches were for people who couldn't make it on their own and they were all a bunch of hypocrites. I thought everybody who believed in healing was sick, everybody who believed in prosperity was broke, and everything seemed to be a sin. Church people all seemed so miserable.

Back then, I sure wasn't looking for God.

But He was looking for me.

And He sent a man into my hotel room one night to tell me so.

CHAPTER 2

He Opened the Ears of My Heart

It was Labor Day Weekend in 1974. I was twenty-five years old, touring with my band playing nineteen-seventies style, kicking rock-n-roll—and I loved it! Man, I *still* love that kind of music! If you saw me back in those days, you'd have called me a "long-haired, hippie freak" unless you were one too! That's what they called guys who looked like me back then.

My hair was chocolate brown and hung down to the middle of my back. I was skinny from using drugs. I had the smell of booze on my breath because I loved to drink. In fact, I drank a bottle of scotch a day—not to get drunk, just because it's what I did. I ran around with women and did as much sinning as I could.

My wife, Cathy, traveled with the band, but she stayed in the hotel room with our daughter, Jodi, most of the time. She tried to make a normal life out of the road. She'd gotten saved about a year and a half before while watching Billy Graham on television, and then she was filled with the Holy Ghost not long after. I couldn't believe it! I'd cuss whenever she'd talk about God so she'd change the subject.

Cathy found a church in every city we went to and attended while we were there. She'd take Jodi to church, and it wasn't long before my two-year-old started telling me I was "going to Hell." It's shocking to hear that come out of a high-pitched little voice!

I'd say, "Who told you that, Jodi?!"

And her little finger would point to Cathy and she'd say, "Mama."

I guess I should have seen it coming because Cathy had been talking to my crazy Pentecostal mama, who was always preaching about God to her. I'd catch Cathy praying over me at night when she thought I was asleep and I'd say, "What are you doing, woman? Are you blankety-blank-blank crazy?! Leave me alone!"

But the life I'd been leading was wearing on me.

That night, I was in my hotel room getting ready to go and play a gig. I happened to finish dressing early and had some time to kill. So I figured I'd watch a little television. Cathy had it tuned to Billy Graham's Labor Day weekend preaching special.

I said, "I ain't watching this junk!"

"Why not?" Cathy said, "He pulls more people than you."

Whoa, Cathy gave me a shot! Normally, she never took pot shots at me, and to this day she says she doesn't know why she said that to me. But it hit home for me and I didn't say anything back because she had a point. I was interested in success, and this guy had filled a stadium with people who wanted to hear what he had to say.

I left him on.

Now, you must understand that back then, I just wasn't what you'd call a nice man. I wasn't friendly or funny. I was ambitious and interested in one thing only—success. I didn't care about anybody but myself. Cathy jokes, "Nobody loved Jesse more than Jesse." She likes to say I was a "legend in my own mind." We laugh about it today because I was such a selfish man, and if things hadn't changed, somebody would be dead today—namely me!

At that time, although I loved my wife, it was my music career that came first and Cathy knew it when she married me. I'd grown up poor, worked since I was eleven, and had a hard life. I came from the old school that says you work hard for everything you get and you don't stop until you get it. Nobody was going to give me anything and I knew it. I had to make a way for myself. That meant that nothing was going to stand in my way—no wife, no kid, no nothing! Everything in life was second to my career.

You wouldn't have liked me back then.

But God loved me.

And as I listened to the preacher on television talk to me about God, I heard something I'd never heard once in all my years in church. I heard about a God Who loved me exactly how I was. He didn't care what I looked like or if I had alcohol on my breath.

That night, I heard about a God Who really cared about me, Who was interested in knowing me, *talking to me,* and Who wanted to wash my sins away and help me out. Now, it's hard to explain, but something happened that night in my heart as I sat there listening. Instead of doing what I'd normally do when Cathy talked to me about God, which was to curse and walk away, I sat still and listened to the man talk. But his words didn't just go into my ears; they went into my heart too.

I'd never felt the compassion of God coming through a preacher's words before, and suddenly I wanted to listen to him talk. I wanted to hear what the man had to say because there was love and mercy in his words. That night, I didn't hear one "don't." I didn't hear about God getting ready to kill me or how much of a low-down, dirty piece of trash I was. I already knew I was a sinner; I didn't need anybody to tell me how bad I was. But I never once heard the preacher say that I wasn't good enough to know God.

As I listened, something started pulling at my heart.

Something started to break.

Now, when you've been pushed down all your life, told that you're not good enough, that you're not worth anything, and that God is angry with you, something happens when you suddenly hear about God's love. Your heart is almost overwhelmed by the love of God. Your mind is almost overwhelmed by the truth.

To suddenly hear that God loves you exactly how you are, that He created your personality, formed you in your mother's womb, and that He cares about you so much that He sent Jesus to die for your sins, well, it is nothing short of amazing.

And that night, I heard that God sent His Son, Jesus, to the cross for me. God wanted to clean me up by washing away my sin so that He could know me and talk to me. And, well, that's all I ever really wanted as a kid. I just wanted a God that I could talk to.

Then I heard the preacher quote this familiar verse:

> *"For God so loved the world, that he gave his only begotten Son, that whosoever believeth in him should not perish, but have everlasting life. For God sent not his Son into the world to condemn the world; but that the world through him might be saved."*

John 3:16,17

In other words, the preacher was saying, "Jesse, God sent Jesus so that you wouldn't die without Him, but that you'd go on after this life to live forever with Him. That's salvation. He didn't send Jesus to condemn you and tell you how bad you are. He sent Him to save you and tell you how much He thinks you're worth."

I suddenly knew that there was a big emptiness inside of me. I'd been living on my own, doing my own thing. I'd been working hard, drinking hard, drugging and living hard. That kind of hard living had molded me into a hard, hard man. But suddenly, that hardness began to crack and the emptiness in my heart was overwhelming.

Now, I'm not a crying kind of man. I couldn't even remember the last time I cried; maybe I was five years old, but I don't really know. I was taught that men just don't cry. Even when I was a very small boy, if I got hurt I was told, "Suck it up, boy! Don't you cry, boy! Be a man!"

As a boy raised in the South, a truck could run over you and you weren't supposed to cry! But my little sister could bruise her toe and wail for hours yet nobody would complain. I never could understand that! Pain is pain, whether you're female or male!

But as I sat there on the edge of the bed, my eyes started filling up. And, because I was so uncomfortable with crying, I got up and went into the bathroom so that Cathy wouldn't see me. As I shut the door, I looked up at the ceiling and tears began to fall from my eyes. I tried to "be a man" and stop the tears, but they wouldn't stop coming. In that bathroom, in Boston, Massachusetts, I released my life into the hands of God.

I said, "God, I don't know if You exist. But if You do, come into my life and save me."

And do you know what happened?

God saved me.

Just like that, I knew in my heart that He had heard my prayer. Now, some people might not believe that, but it is true. It's hard to explain, but it was like a giant pressure came off of my chest. I suddenly knew without a shadow of doubt that God was real, that He was right there listening to me, and that He had just answered my prayer by coming into my heart. He was filling me up with Himself and healing me. Suddenly, I wasn't on my own anymore. I had God.

It was a simple prayer, but it radically changed my life and I walked out that bathroom a free man. I didn't even know that I was carrying such heavy burden. I didn't have a clue that I was a prisoner in my own life. But after I accepted God, I realized for the first time that I was free, really free, and that God Himself loved me. Life suddenly felt new. I walked out of that hotel bathroom a new man.

I had been born again.

Man, who would have thought it could happen to me?! Nobody but Cathy and my mama! And, of course, God. He knew I needed Him all along. He knew all about my past and was waiting for me to turn to Him so that He could show me a good future. God had plans for my life that I couldn't have dreamed up if I'd tried!

A Voice Coming from My Heart

When I got born again that night in Boston, I immediately began to notice that something had really changed in my heart. It was as if God had put ears in my heart, and suddenly I was hearing this still, small voice talking to me.

In the days following my commitment, I'd wake up in the middle of the night and I'd hear this voice coming from my heart. At first I didn't know what was going on, but soon I realized that the voice coming from my heart was God. He was talking to me!

Before I accepted Jesus as my Savior, I never heard a voice coming from my heart. I didn't even hear the "voice of conscience" as people call it. I didn't have a conscience that I knew of! I sinned without a second thought and I figured that the more sin I could do, the better. I did whatever made me feel good for the moment. It didn't matter if it was sleeping with a different girl or two every night, drinking bottles of whiskey, or snorting cocaine for fun.

I used to sprinkle hallucinogenics in the club's popcorn bins and then laugh as people got so loaded that they fell off barstools. I could have killed them if they were taking other drugs, but I didn't care. I was crazy and without conscience.

But after I gave my life to God, my heart completely changed. It was as if blinders had been taken off of my eyes and I could see, really see, for the first time in my life. I'll never forget it because I had to play a show the night I got saved, and when I walked into the club, I looked around and saw it for what it was—a pit. It was a dark, red velvet-covered pit. I played my show because it was my job and I was on contract, but my heart wasn't in it.

I still liked the music, but the lifestyle wasn't attractive at all to me. I didn't want to drink anymore. I didn't want to dishonor my wife by sleeping with other women. I wanted to be loyal to her and be a good father to my baby girl. I didn't want to snort cocaine, take PCP, or swallow speed. God had changed my heart. He'd given me a desire for purity that I'd never had before. And I began to have a love for people, too, that I never had before.

Suddenly, I cared about my band members' souls! I couldn't have cared less what they believed in before. But now, I wanted them to know that God was real. They didn't care too much to hear about it though. They would hear me and just agree for agreement's sake. They'd say, "Yeah, man. Jesus, man. That's cool."

They were just like I was before God changed my heart. We all had a 1960s attitude that was basically, "Whatever is good for you is good for you and whatever is good for me is good for me." But suddenly, I knew differently.

God was for everybody and not just for me. I knew I had to get out of the rock music industry. My heart wasn't there, and I knew God had other plans for my life.

It's a Joy Knowing God

I went through many changes during those early years of my life and today I am a preacher of the Gospel. I never thought that would happen! Nobody else did either! I'm the last guy my family, or anyone else who knew me, expected to become a preacher. When I went to my high school reunion, I was the one voted "Most Changed." It wasn't an understatement! I've changed completely from the man I used to be.

God called me to be a preacher in 1976, and since then He's used-me to show other people that being saved isn't a drag. It can be fun. I-don't believe that you have to suddenly become a religious fanatic when you get saved, although I've seen a lot of people who seem do that!

Being saved means that you are aware of the reality of God, His plan of salvation, and the importance of communicating with your Father. When I got saved, God's book, the Bible, suddenly became important to me. I wanted to know what God had to say! My eyes were open to see truth. When a person gets saved, the ears of their hearts are opened to hear truth.

I believe that living for God isn't some hardship you have to endure. I think it is a joy to know God. It's fun waking up in the morning and talking to God. I'm never really alone because God is always with me, He's ready to teach me from His Word and talk to me—even guide me in life—so that I make the right decisions.

I believe that everyone can talk to God and fully expect Him to communicate back. It starts when you decide to release your life to God like I did in 1974. When you understand that Christ died on the cross for you and ask God to save you, it's as though He puts ears on your heart right then so you can hear Him say, "Of course I will save you. I am not willing for anyone to perish but that all would come to Me and have everlasting life."

Later on in the book, I will go through the many different ways God speaks to us using biblical examples and my own experiences. I've found that God uses all sorts of ways to get through to us! He uses the Bible, visions, dreams, the inner witness, the gifts of the Holy Spirit—even His audible voice—and a lot of odd ways too! But-before all that, I must share with you the basics of getting to know God.

Without really knowing the Lord, you can't hear His voice. Or, you may be hearing His voice and not even realizing He is talking to you. Either way, these next few chapters are going to help you understand some things about salvation, God, Jesus, and the Holy Spirit so that you can lay a strong foundation for hearing His wonderful voice.

CHAPTER 3

God Made Our Connection Simple

The word *saved* is so strange to some people because they just don't understand what it is that they actually get saved from when they give their lives to God. Hell is hot and nobody wants to go there, but we also get saved from the terrible feeling of being separated from God, which hurts us the most in this life.

Before Jesus died for our sins, that sin caused a separation to come between God and mankind. The sin-separation was like a thick wall that kept us from easily accessing our Father. When we accept Jesus, that wall crumbles and suddenly we're not separated from our Father anymore.

God made us. We're His kids and we're created to communicate with Him. In the book of Genesis, you can read about how Adam communicated with God freely before sin came into the earth. God literally walked in the Garden of Eden in the cool of the day with man! Then the wall of sin came down and that really messed the world up.

Today, God is in Heaven. But He is still our Father, and He doesn't want us to be like lost orphans wandering around without

---

knowing Who our Daddy is. Everybody needs a father in life. It's part of God's family plan. Now, if you didn't have a dad who hung around, or if you had a dad that hung around but you wished hadn't because he was so terrible, let me give you some words of peace: You've got a good Father in God. He is not an abuser or a loser!

If we are separated from God, we're alone. That separation is what gives people the feeling that they have a "void" in their lives. The void is simply life without God; that is why someone can be in a room full of people or have a family the size of Texas and still feel completely alone.

If you feel that void, you need God to get rid of it. You do that by simply accepting that you need Him in your life, believing in His plan of salvation through Jesus Christ, and releasing your life into His hands. It can be as simple as saying, "God, I give myself to You." That's what I did. Remember, God is not waiting for you to say some beautiful prayer. The most beautiful prayer you can pray is the one that you really mean in your heart.

People Make It Hard, God Made It Simple

In the New Testament book of Romans, there are a few passages that tell you how to get saved. You should look the passages up in your own Bible if you haven't already read them before, so you'll see how the Bible says it.

"That if thou shalt confess with thy mouth the Lord Jesus, and shalt believe in thine heart that God hath raised him from the dead, thou shalt be saved.

"For with the heart man believeth unto righteousness; and with the mouth confession is made unto salvation.

"For the Scripture saith, Whosoever believeth on him shall not be ashamed.

"For there is no difference between the Jew and the Greek: for the same Lord over all is rich unto all that call upon him.

"For whosoever shall call upon the name of the Lord shall be saved."

Romans 10:9-13

In other words, it just takes saying with your mouth that you need God and believing it in your heart to gain salvation. It doesn't matter what nationality, gender, or race you are because the same Lord is over everybody. Everyone can ask God to come into their life, and they'll be saved according to that Scripture.

Salvation is so simple. I don't know why people make it hard! Sometimes people want to put you through all kinds of rituals, but it's not necessary. All it takes to be saved is a sincere heart, faith, and acceptance of God's plan of salvation through Jesus. That's it.

People might try to make it hard, but God doesn't want to keep anybody out of Heaven. It's not an exclusive club. He loves all of us, including you, and wants to be a part of our lives. He wants us to live with Him as our Father during our lifetime so that we have guidance, peace, joy, and love. Then when we die, He wants to take us to a special place He's created for us.

All we have to do is pray and release our lives to God, and He will come into our hearts and save us. Some people like to pray a specific prayer because it helps to guide them along as they pray. I put a prayer of salvation at the end of this book just in case you want to use it. It may help you, or help you to lead someone else to a new life in Christ. It will help you to be born again, just like I am.

The term *born again* scares some people, but it isn't a new term. It is as old as the New Testament of the Bible. In fact, Jesus made it popular when He was talking to a man named Nicodemus. This guy was a ruler over the Jews, and you can read the whole story for yourself in the third chapter of the Gospel of John.

Nicodemus was afraid people would find out that he was talking to Jesus, so he came at nighttime so no one would see him. Here's his conversation with Jesus:

"...Rabbi, we know that thou art a teacher come from God: for no man can do these miracles that thou doest, except God be with him.

"Jesus answered and said unto him, Verily, verily, I say unto thee, Except a man be born again, he cannot see the kingdom of God."

John 3:2,3

Jesus told Nicodemus how to be sure to see the kingdom of God by telling him that we must be born again. This is why Christians use that term.

Nicodemus didn't have a clue what Jesus was talking about. He said, and I'll paraphrase, "What? I have to climb back up into my mama's womb or something?"

"Jesus answered, Verily, verily, I say unto thee, Except a man be born of water and of the Spirit, he cannot enter into the kingdom of God.

"That which is born of the flesh is flesh; and that which is born of the Spirit is spirit.

"Marvel not that I said unto thee, Ye must be born again."

John 3:5-7

Then Jesus went on to talk about the mystery of salvation, comparing it to the blowing wind. We hear the sound of the wind, but-we can't really tell where it's coming from or where it's going. Jesus says that's the way it is with those who are born of the Spirit (v.-8). In other words, God is a big God and His ways are mysterious, but the truth of the matter is that you must be spiritually reborn in order to experience the kingdom of God.

> *"Nicodemus answered and said unto him, How can these things be?*
>
> *"Jesus answered and said unto him, Art thou a master of Israel, and knowest not these things?"*
>
> John 3:9,10

In other words, Jesus was saying, "You're a ruler over the Jews, Nico! Why don't you know this stuff?"

Jesus goes on to say,

> *"Verily, verily, I say unto thee, We speak that we do know, and testify that we have seen; and ye receive not our witness.*
>
> *"If I have told you earthly things, and ye believe not, how shall ye believe, if I tell you of heavenly things?*
>
> *"And no man hath ascended up to heaven, but He that came down from heaven, even the Son of man which is in heaven.*
>
> *"And as Moses lifted up the serpent in the wilderness, even so must the Son of man be lifted up."*
>
> John 3:11-14

This is where Jesus is telling Nicodemus about the cross. He says, and this is my paraphrase, "Just like Moses lifted up the serpent on the cross, so I, the Son of Man, am about to be lifted up on a cross."

Then Jesus tells what will take place when people see or hear about Him lifted up on that cross:

"That whosoever believeth in him should not perish, but have eternal life.

"For God so loved the world, that he gave his only begotten Son, that whosoever believeth in him should not perish, but have everlasting life."

John 3:15,16

That's the message of salvation right there. It's Jesus' message, not mine! Jesus goes on to say in verse seventeen,

*"For God sent not his Son into the world to condemn the world; but that the world through him might be **saved**."*

John 3:17

In other words, God didn't send Jesus to earth so that all of us would feel like low-down, dirty pieces of trash. He sent His only Son so we'd know we were loved! He didn't send Jesus to condemn us! He sent Jesus to save us! Then Jesus continues:

"He that believeth on Him is not condemned: but he that believeth not is condemned already, because he hath not believed in the name of the only begotten Son of God."

John 3:18

This was Jesus' explanation about the difference between unbelievers and believers. He said that people who believe in His sacrifice on the cross aren't condemned because of it. They're saved because of their faith. But those who don't believe are already condemned because of their choice not to believe that He is really God's only Son.

Some people think that they can scoot through life without choosing sides. But this Scripture is saying, "Look, you're already condemned unless you choose to believe in God's Son." Until a person chooses Jesus, they are living condemned lives. That's only because until we choose Jesus, we remain separated from God; but it's so simple to choose Jesus. I don't know why everyone doesn't do it! But some don't, and that's what Jesus starts talking about next.

> *"And this is the condemnation, that light is come into the world, and men loved darkness rather than light, because their deeds were evil.*
>
> *"For every one that doeth evil hateth the light, neither cometh to the light, lest his deeds should be reproved."*
>
> John 3:19-20

In other words, the reason some people don't come to Jesus is because they like doing bad deeds and don't want anybody to tell them to stop doing what they're doing. The interesting thing is that once a person gives their life over to God, their heart changes and they don't really want to do bad deeds anymore. The desires of their hearts just change.

That's what happened to me and to countless thousands of people that I've preached to over the years. I've heard story after story of this happening to people. A person who sincerely reaches out to God for salvation and wants God's hand to move in their life will experience that radical change of heart.

Jesus continues,

> *"But he that doeth truth cometh to the light, that his deeds may be made manifest, that they are wrought in God."*
>
> John 3:21

When individuals are living in truth, they want their deeds to be noticed because they know that each of those deeds is a reflection of God's hand in their life. Once people get saved and start living the Christian life, they want to share their joy and knowledge with others.

Beginning Again

The *born again* term that Jesus used in talking with Nicodemus means that once people accept that God loves them and that He sent His Son to get rid of their sin, their old lives end and they get to start over, just like being born again.

At the first birth, it's a physical manifestation of new life. The second birth, or new birth, is a spiritual manifestation of new life. We are brand new again because our heart has been changed, our eyes have been opened, and we're able to hear the voice of our Father God.

Second Corinthians 5:17 says this: *"Therefore if any man be in Christ, he is a new creature: old things are passed away; behold, all things are become new."* You might want to memorize that if you don't know it already. That'll help you out.

When it comes to salvation, I always say, "If you don't like the way you were born, try it again." Jesus is God's way of giving people-a clean slate. And who doesn't need that? Nobody's perfect. You would be Jesus if you were perfect, and there is only one of Him! The Bible says that His name would be called "Emmanuel."

Do you know what the name *Emmanuel* means?

It means "God with us."

Isn't that great? God was so interested in being around us that He chose to come down to earth as a man—a man named Jesus Christ.

CHAPTER 4

Emmanuel, God with Us

Mary was a young girl who was engaged to a guy named Joseph, and she was a virgin. Biblical scholars have put her age at about fifteen years old. Before Mary was even married or had sexual relations with her fiancé Joseph, she was *"...found with child of the Holy Ghost"* (Matthew 1:18). So, we know who Jesus' Daddy was— and it wasn't Joseph.

Now, if you're engaged and your woman tells you she's pregnant but you didn't have anything to do with it, how are you going to react? Probably not like Joseph. *"Then Joseph her husband, being a just man and not willing to make her a public example, was minded to put her away privately"* (Matthew 1:19).

Now, Joseph was a pretty good old boy. If I was Joseph and my girlfriend came up to me and said, "Honey, I'm pregnant but it's not what you think. Sweetie, it's an immaculate conception," I don't think I would have believed her. I mean, I was born at night but not last night! I'd "put her away," alright—it's called splitsville! Like most people, I would have probably broken off that engagement and let her go on her way.

Joseph didn't do that. But the Bible says that at night, he was thinking about it. I guess so! I would be too! He was probably thinking to himself, *Man, I know she wants me to believe it, but I've got to sleep on this!* God saw that Joseph was thinking about it and sent an angel to talk to him in a dream—this is one of the ways God speaks to people.

Of course, God knew He had to tell the boy something, because it was just inconceivable for a woman to get pregnant without the aid of a man's sperm. You've just got to have that if you want a baby! Here's how the Bible tells the story:

> *"But while he thought on these things, behold, the angel of the Lord appeared unto him in a dream, saying, Joseph, thou son of David, fear not to take unto thee Mary thy wife: for that which is conceived in her is **of the Holy Ghost.***

> *"And she shall bring forth a Son, and thou shalt call his name JESUS: for he shall save his people from their sins.*

> *"Now all this was done, that it might be fulfilled which was spoken of the Lord by the prophet, saying,*

> *"Behold, a virgin shall be with child, and shall bring forth a son, and they shall call his name Emmanuel, which being interpreted is, **God with us.***

> *"Then Joseph being raised from sleep did as the angel of the Lord had bidden him, and took unto him his wife:*

> *"And knew her not till she had brought forth her firstborn son: and he called his name **JESUS.**"*

> Matthew 1:20-25

Notice that in God's eyes, Mary is Joseph's wife because they were promised to one another, and under Jewish custom, once you were promised you were almost as good as married. God saw it as a union that was meant to be even though they hadn't sealed the union yet with a ceremony. This was a God-ordained union; God set this family up. He not only chose Mary to be Jesus' mother, but He chose Joseph to be Jesus' father on earth, to care for His Son and train Him as a child.

Fatherhood is very important to God. He didn't need Joseph's sperm, but He did need Joseph's fatherly influence. God chose Joseph, who was such an honorable man that he stayed with Mary even though it was completely against all logic and reason for her to be pregnant from the Holy Spirit of God. So, Joseph not only had faith in Mary's word, but he also had faith in the voice of God—which came to Him in the form of a dream.

When the angel said, *"For that which is conceived in her is of the-Holy Ghost,"* you don't hear Joseph arguing about it. He accepted it as-a fact, got up, and started his role as Jesus' daddy. He took some responsibility even though the kid wasn't his. Man, there's a lesson in-that!

The Virginity of Mary

The Holy Spirit of God was Jesus' biological father. Some people are debating this today. The hermeneutical, philosophical, theological scholars are debating the word *virgin* in the Bible, and some say that Mary wasn't really a virgin. They say that the word *virgin* simply means "young maiden." There are always people trying to discount Jesus' birth, life, and death.

There were a lot of young maidens who had babies, but the bottom line is that Mary had a baby without the aid of a man. That virgin aspect of the birth isn't mentioned once and dismissed, it's repeated over and over again. We were warned that it was going to happen in Isaiah 7:14 in the Old Testament, *"Therefore the Lord himself shall give you a sign; Behold, a virgin shall conceive, and bear a son, and shall call his name Immanuel."*

Then it happens in the New Testament in Matthew 1:23, *"Behold, a virgin shall be with child, and shall bring forth a son, and they shall call his name Emmanuel, which being interpreted is, God with us."*

Then the story is repeated in Luke about how the angel visited Mary before she was pregnant and told her that it was going to happen.

"To a virgin espoused to a man whose name was Joseph, of the house of David; and the virgin's name was Mary.

"And the angel came in unto her, and said, Hail, thou that art highly favored, the Lord is with thee: blessed art thou among women.

"And when she saw him, she was troubled at his saying, and cast in her mind what manner of salutation this should be.

"And the angel said unto her, Fear not, Mary: for thou hast found favor with God.

"And, behold, thou shalt conceive in thy womb, and bring forth a son, and shalt call his name JESUS.

"He shall be great, and shall be called the Son of the Highest: and the Lord God shall give unto him the throne of his father David:

"And he shall reign over the house of Jacob for ever; and of his kingdom there shall be no end."

Luke 1:27-33

The best part of this passage about Mary being a virgin is when Mary responded to the angel.

"Then said Mary unto the angel, How shall this be, **seeing I know not a man?**

*"And the angel answered and said unto her, The Holy Ghost shall come upon thee, and the power of the Highest shall overshadow thee: therefore also **that holy thing which shall be born of thee shall be called the Son of God.***

"And, behold, thy cousin Elisabeth, she hath also conceived a son in her old age: and this is the sixth month with her, who was called barren.

"For with God nothing shall be impossible.

"And Mary said, Behold the handmaid of the Lord; be it unto me according to thy word. And the angel departed from her."

Luke 1:34-38

Don't let anyone ever tell you Mary wasn't a virgin! It's plain as day, regardless of whatever word study they're doing this time around.-The Scripture tells the story of a miracle birth. If it was just some girl who got pregnant out of wedlock, do you think we'd be talking about it today? No. Jesus' life started off as a miracle. Then, He lived a miraculous life—free of sin according to Hebrews 4:15. He-did miracles that are described throughout the Gospels and the New Testament. And through His death, we can obtain the miracle of-salvation.

God Isn't Against Us

Emmanuel doesn't mean "God against us."

It doesn't mean "God trying to hurt us."

It doesn't mean "God with us sometimes, maybe if He feels like it."

No, it means "God with us"!

To a lot of people, hearing that Jesus was born is just a Christmas story. But it happened and the "God with us" message is the central theme of Christianity. At Christmas, people read the story of the angel who spoke to the nearby shepherds when Jesus was born.

"And the angel said unto them, Fear not: for, behold, I bring you good tidings of great joy, which shall be to all people.

"For unto you is born this day in the city of David a Saviour, which is Christ the Lord.

"And this shall be a sign unto you; Ye shall find the babe wrapped in swaddling clothes, lying in a manger.

"And suddenly there was with the angel a multitude of the heavenly host praising God, and saying,

"Glory to God in the highest, and on earth peace, good will toward men."

Luke 2:10-14

That day, angels were praising God because something new had happened. There was some serious joy being spread around in the sky that day. The Bible called it tidings of *great* joy.

Where's the Joy in an Absent Jesus?

It's not joyful for you and me today to just know that Jesus came. I'm glad He came, but what about the generations that came after Jesus' time? If He's not here for us now, how can the fact that He once came help us in the reality of day-to-day life?

As long as I can remember, the church has been preaching what I call an "absent Jesus." They focus on the fact that He came. They focus on the fact that He died and rose again. But what I always wanted to know about was how that Good News could affect my everyday life.

If you're curious like I was, here is the Good News: He has made a way for you to know God, talk to Him, and fully expect Him to talk back. Salvation through Jesus Christ opens the airwaves, so to speak. He opens the communication lines so that you can talk to God and He can talk back to you.

God talks to us in many ways. Once I got born again, I started doing research on it and found many different ways God speaks to His people. Now, whether we're listening or not is a whole different matter!

Do you ever wonder what it would be like if you said, "Jesus," and He went, "What?" When I was a kid, if that would have happened, I would have hollered out loud, "He said something!"

That's what "God with us" means. "God away from us" would mean that He never talks. But that's just not true. The apostles would not have won men to God if they had preached an absent Jesus. And yet all through my religious upbringing, I served an absent Jesus. All that I wanted was a God that I could talk to. But nobody would let me.

If you told them, "I'm waiting for an answer," they'd say, "Now, don't be stupid!"

The great secret of Christian joy lies in the fact that we believe in a present Jesus, not an absent Jesus. We believe in a God Who is with us, not away from us. After you are born again, you read the Bible and get to know what He said. You pray and get used to talking to Him. If you listen, you'll hear His voice in your heart talking back.

Today when I say, "Jesus," He says, "Jesse."

If you can't imagine that God would talk to you like that, guess what? He won't. You've got to believe it first, because that's how everything with God works. First you believe, then you receive. That's how you get saved, so that's how it works when you talk to God too.

If He Talks to Me, He Will Talk to You

The God I serve is accessible. I know He's with me and that He stands beside me as I go through this life. When everything is coming against me, I know that God is still with me and that I don't have to worry or fret for anything. My God hears me when I pray.

I have preached all over America and in many countries throughout the world. Just about every place I can think of, I've been told, "Brother Jesse, I would just love to hear God talk to me like He talks to you." People want to hear from Jesus.

I say, "I know that if He talks to me, then He will talk to you! He's no respecter of persons." According to the Bible, God believes in equality. Romans 2:11 plainly says, *"For there is no respect of persons with God."*

And there are many more Scriptures that reiterate this, such as 2-Chronicles 19:7, Acts 10:34, Ephesians 6:9, Colossians 3:24-25, and-James 2:1. God is a fair and just Father, and He wants you to hear His voice.

He's not an absent Father.

He's a present Spirit.

CHAPTER 5

God Is a Spirit

One reason people have a hard time hearing God's voice is because they try to communicate with Him with their mind or their body, when God is a Spirit. The Bible says in John 4:24 that *"God is a Spirit: and they that worship him must worship him in spirit and in truth."* Hearing God's voice is one of the perks of having a relationship with God. Hearing God's voice happens when your new, re-born spirit communicates with God's Holy Spirit.

Who is the Holy Spirit? The Holy Spirit is an amazing facet of God's Holy Trinity. He's the One Who moved over the deep in Genesis and responded to the Father's commands during creation.

He isn't a bird.

Some people read that passage in the Bible where John the Baptist was baptizing Jesus and the Holy Spirit descended on Jesus like a dove (John 1:32) and they think that a bird really landed on Jesus' head! The Holy Spirit descended on Him *like* a dove, but it doesn't say it was an actual dove landing on His holy head!

The Holy Spirit is part of the Holy Trinity of God the Father, God the Son, and God the Holy Spirit. The Father is an orderly God. He set up a divine chain of command that we are supposed to follow in order to easily and quickly speak with Him.

The Divine Chain of Command

The divine chain of command begins with the Father. He's the "Head Honcho," in charge over everything. Next comes Jesus. He's God's only Son and the mediator between God and man. Then comes the Holy Spirit Who flows all over the world. To make it easy to understand, I often give an analogy explaining the Godhead in relation to the outward appearance of a physical body.

I say, "The heart of God is the Father. The face of God is the Son, Jesus. The voice of God is the Holy Spirit." What are we? We are the hands of God. Each of us are God's hands in this earth. It's up to us to fulfill His plan in the earth, to love and treat people as we want to be loved and treated.

Everything begins with the Father, because He is the first in the Trinity. Then, the second person of the Trinity is the Son. The third person of the Trinity is the Holy Ghost, Who has many names. They are all called God, because they are all parts or expressions of God. The Father is one part of God, the Son is one part of God, and the Holy Spirit is one part of God. Together we call them the "God-head" or simply the Holy Trinity (tri meaning three) of God.

God is One. He is not many gods. He is one God with three expressions—the Father, the Son, and the Holy Ghost! Now, how God can be three and yet be one is the mystery of the Holy Trinity. It's hard for us to understand exactly how it happens with our own mind because it's a true spiritual concept, but according to the Bible, these are actually the three parts of God; so it's just something you accept by faith.

That Trinity also works under a divine chain of command when it comes to hearing God's voice. Messages are birthed within the Father and He speaks it to the Son. The Son relays it to the Holy Spirit, which then relays it to your spirit. However that message comes, we must realize that it begins in the heart of the Father!

The Way God Works

You must realize that the Father and the Son aren't the Ones Who are on the earth. Although the Holy Trinity is united, these two members aren't the ones actively working on earth. They are seated at the throne in Heaven together. According to Hebrews 12:2, Jesus is sitting at His right hand. *"Looking unto Jesus the author and finisher of our faith; who for the joy that was set before him endured the cross, despising the shame, **and is set down at the right hand of the throne of God.**"*

Although God the Father, God the Son, and God the Holy Spirit are unified and work together as one unit, it is the Holy Spirit Who is actively working upon the earth today. The Holy Spirit of God does so much on the earth. I can't begin to describe everything He does! But I-will tell you some of the main things He has done and is continuing to do.

The Holy Spirit acted upon God's commands during creation. He inspired the Scriptures we have today. People in the Old Testament who sought after God with their hearts were made able to hear His voice by way of the Holy Spirit.

Old Testament men of God prophesied God's plans for people's lives and in the future by way of the Holy Spirit too. The Holy Spirit would come and rest upon people who sought after God. He would impart wisdom to them, comfort them, instruct them, and generally help them out in life. The Holy Spirit is the third person of the Trinity Who anointed all Old Testament prophets of God to lead the people.

Isaiah and Joel spoke of the day when the Holy Spirit would be poured out on every believer who wanted Him and His gifts would be used among believers everywhere. Check out Joel 2:28-32 and Acts 2:17-21 to learn more about that. Since the beginning of time, it has been the Holy Spirit Who brought conviction to the hearts of people when they were doing wrong.

Since Jesus went to the cross, it is the Holy Spirit Who comes to live within people who accept Him as Savior and Lord. This is the miracle of the new birth.

After salvation, it is the Holy Spirit Who gives the gifts of the Spirit and fruit of the Spirit to help people to grow and mature, and to help the church as a whole to grow and mature also.

The sacrifice Jesus made at the cross was what made it possible for you to have the Holy Spirit literally dwelling within you. While the Holy Spirit is God's voice in the earth and the convictor of your heart before salvation, He isn't your mediator to God. That is Jesus' job! He earned it by going to the cross to die for your sins.

That's why we call Jesus the mediator to the Father, and that's why you hear so many people pray "in Jesus' name" at the end of their prayers. As the mediator to God, Jesus is extremely important because without Jesus, you aren't going to be able to hear from God's active messenger, the Holy Spirit.

What Is the Truth?

*"Jesus saith unto him, **I am** the way, **the truth**, and the
life: no man cometh unto the Father, but by me."* John 14:6

Jesus is the truth. Nobody can rightly go to His Father, God,
unless they first go through Him. Again, that's why you hear people
pray "in-the name of Jesus." It's the right thing to do.

John 1:14 further points to Jesus as being full of *truth* when it
says, *"And the Word was made flesh, and dwelt among us, (and we
beheld his glory, the glory as of the only begotten of the Father,) full
of grace and truth."*

The most famous Scripture about truth is probably this one:
"And-ye shall know the truth, and the truth shall make you free"
(John-8:32). How many times have you heard someone use that
Scripture? Even people who know nothing about God quote it! Why?
Because it's a fact. When you know the truth, you are set free in
whatever area you apply that truth. Your mind is set free from lies,
delusion, or denial.

The truth in God's Word will set you free from the bondage
of your past. If you allow it to do this by reading its teachings and
communicating with God, the truth of God's Word will set you free
from those old issues that you may be harboring. Those things we
hold onto from our past keep us down in life. They stand in our way
from moving on and being the best we can be.

God wants us to be the best we can be. That's His plan for us! He
loved us enough to send Jesus, so we can know Him and allow Him to
guide us and help us out in life. That's the way God works! Spiritually
speaking, it's the truth of Jesus' redemptive work that sets all who

accept it free from that wall of sin that once stood between them and God.

Now, a lot of people today try to argue with the fact that Jesus is the only mediator to God. They may say, "There are many paths to God." But according to the Bible's teachings, Jesus is the only mediator between God and man. It's everyone's free will to choose whether to believe that or not.

I believe that while there have been many great moral teachers in history, Jesus was the only Son of God. He is the only redeemer of man. You can't visit Him at a grave site somewhere because He rose from the dead. His body isn't lying within this earth. He was God Who walked in the flesh, making a way for you and I to talk to God. His blood sacrifice is the only one that God will accept.

When we accept Jesus, God accepts us.

When we accept Jesus, the Holy Spirit comes to live in us.

That's God's plan. That's how we gain access to Him, get His Spirit within us, and suddenly have the ability to hear His voice.

You Can't Put God in a Box

But while this is the divine chain of command, you can't put God in a box and say He only works this way. He may follow the chain of command most of the time, but sometimes He just flexes His sovereignty and does something different. Sovereignty basically means that God is God and He can do whatever He wants to do. Sometimes people use this as an excuse for situations that they don't understand, but I believe that God obeys His own Word all the time.

He's not a liar. He said in Psalms 89:34, *"My covenant will I not break, nor alter the thing that is gone out of my lips."* In other words,

"I'm not breaking My promises and I'm not changing what I say. You can count on Me."

If you believe that God doesn't keep His Word, then the sovereignty doctrine that says "You know how God is, sometimes He does and then sometimes He doesn't…" might make sense to you. But if you believe, like I do, that God is a just and righteous God, then that "sometimes He does, sometimes He doesn't" doctrine just falls to pieces with even the smallest amount of Scripture. There's a whole book called the Bible that attests to God's faithfulness to His Word!

The truth is that God is sovereign and has unlimited power. Yet He has chosen to limit Himself to what He will and will not do concerning mankind. He spelled it out in His Word. And that makes Him sovereign, outside of what He said in His Word.

Can God do anything? Yes. Will God do anything? No. God has already said what He will do in many situations. He's already laid the plan out pretty plain. He has bound Himself with His own Word and that's what makes Him trustworthy.

We know that He can't lie because of Titus 1:2, and we know the father of all lies is the devil because of John 8:44. Yet people still talk about God as if He breaks promises on a whim. This is not true. God is a promise-keeper, not a promise-breaker. If the Bible says God said something, you can take it to the bank that He means it and He's not backing off of what He said.

God will follow through. We're the ones who usually don't follow through, and then we have problems that we blame on God's sovereignty. Maybe we lack knowledge or wisdom in a certain area and because we don't know, we figure it's God's fault. But He won't sway from His Word.

But if something is not in God's Word, well, that's a whole other story! God is a sovereign Being and can do whatever He wants to in situations that fall outside the boundaries of His Word.

What Is a Sovereign Act of God?

So, what exactly is a sovereign act of God then? The perfect example of a sovereign act of God is the story of Saul of Tarsus on the road to Damascus. This incident has nothing to do with God's already established Word. God decides to do something to get Saul's attention. You can read Acts chapter 9 if you want to know the full story.

Basically what happens is this. Saul decides he is going to kill some Christians. The Bible says he's so ticked off that he's *"... breathing out threatenings and slaughter against the disciples of the Lord"* (Acts 9:1). The boy is mad and he's looking to hurt somebody. The Lord decides to intervene. God slaps him off his donkey, shines a light around him, and starts talking audibly to Saul.

I'll paraphrase, "Why are you persecuting Me, Saul?"

Saul is blown away by this and says, "Who are you, Lord?"

"I'm Jesus, the One you're persecuting!"

"OK, Lord. What do You want me to do?"

God tells him to go to the city and he will be told what to do when he gets there. That begins the life of Saul who became Paul, who would soon become an apostle of the Lord Jesus Christ—the one who would become the preacher to the Gentiles.

Now, that situation was a sovereign act of God. That's God doing something outside of what He's already said in His Word— not inside. The Bible never promised us that God would shine a light around every one of us while we're traveling down the road and tell us to stop doing what we're doing! God doesn't slap everybody who's mad and riding a donkey to persecute Christians. No, this was a special incident where God acted sovereignly outside of His Word and did what He wanted to do.

You might have heard stories about people being saved supernaturally from accidents and that kind of thing. Those are strange occurrences and often happen because God acts sovereignly outside of His Word. Why does He do that? I don't know why, but I think we'll find out His reasons when we get to Heaven.

I had a sovereign thing happen to me one time when I saw God with my own eyes and heard Him with my own ears. I got saved in 1974. From that time I started reading the Word a lot, and if there was one thing I noticed, it was that God showed Himself to people in the Bible. He talked out loud to them.

CHAPTER 6

"Why Can't You Talk to Me, God?"

Once I got saved, I began to wonder, "Why can't God talk to me like He did to those guys in the Bible? Why can't I hear His voice out loud?" For the first two years I was saved, this was a big concern for me. It was on my mind every time I read a Scripture where God talked to somebody or God showed Himself to someone. God was already speaking to my spirit in His still, small voice. But I was interested in hearing Him with my ears, audibly. For two years, I really sought after this.

The First Few Years

During the first few years after I got born again, I wasn't a preacher. Some people think you get saved, then God throws you into ministry. God doesn't throw babies into the field of ministry. The pastors, prophets, teachers, preachers, and evangelists are God's executive branch. He trains them in His Word and helps them to wise up before He sends them out to teach His kids!

During these first few years, I had a regular job. When God saved me from a life of alcohol and drugs, He removed my desire to play music in the bars and clubs. It wasn't long before I had to leave the music industry. I decided to go back home to Southern Louisiana so that my daughter, Jodi, could get to know the rest of the family.

Jodi had spent her first four years in hotel rooms across America with Cathy, sleeping during the day and staying up at night. She'd ride her tricycle down the halls at two in the morning! Jodi was on the typical rock musician's schedule, and she wasn't able to be around other kids unless another kid happened to be at the music store or the laundromat. Those were her favorite places! That kid's birthday parties were filled with hippies and rock-n-roll band members. We drank scotch while she drank fruit punch, and everybody had a good time eating the birthday cake! But I wanted her to have a more normal life. So we moved back to Southern Louisiana, and I suddenly had to find a job.

Now, I'd grown up playing music. That's what I knew how to do best and felt very confident about it. After I left this industry, I didn't know what kind of work to do. But I knew that God had done a mighty work in my life and that He'd given me a chance at a new life, and for this I was eternally grateful. Even though I didn't really know what to do, I was confident that God would help me start again.

When I came back to Louisiana, I looked for work. I wouldn't go back to the clubs for anything! Many people questioned my choice of leaving the music industry where I made good money. Even my own dad told me I was crazy to leave the music business. But for me, it was about the principle. Sometimes it can be hard on a man's pride to take work that he once looked down on to stick to his principles. But I feel that it's much harder on your mind to compromise what you know is right for the sake of money.

I decided that the only thing to do was to put my faith in Him. So I prayed and told Jesus that if He'd help me find a job, anything to support my family, I'd continue to share my testimony and be a good example of a life turned around by the hand of God.

Right after that prayer, I found work with a trucking company. My job was to sell drilling pipe to oil companies. The job didn't pay anywhere near what I made playing music, and it was entirely different than anything I'd ever done before. But, I was so excited to be the will of God that I readily accepted the challenge and did my job with a good heart.

I worked hard for that company, tithed to my church, and God honored me. He gave me favor with my bosses, and because they liked my work and noticed I had a "whatever it takes" attitude, they chose to promote me.

Meanwhile, I had enough money to support my family and enjoy my life with them, all the while using my musical talents for Him. I led the choir at my church, and man, that was one kickin' choir! I'm sharing this to show you that when you give your life to God and you're faithful to Him, He will take care of you—even if you don't know what to do with your own life.

Then God opened another door. He gave me a great opportunity to go to work for one of the oil companies I'd been selling pipe to, Shell Oil Company, and I spent a few years at this company. I loved my job and planned to be there for a very long time. But life takes all sorts of turns and twists. One day God called me out of the oil field and into the ministry. I felt like I was starting the cycle all over again!

What would I do? I didn't know how to be a preacher! I could play music and sing. I could buy and sell pipeline, furnishing oil rigs with pipe for drilling—but a preacher?! That's the last thing I wanted to do and the last thing I thought I could do.

I'm Cajun. My way of talking isn't like other preachers. I thought, *Will anybody ever listen to or respect a Cajun preacher?* But God called me and I knew it. I'd heard His voice and knew that ministry was where I belonged, even though most preachers I knew thought I wasn't "ministry material."

But I knew I had to obey God's voice, regardless if I was the right kind of preacher or not. Even if no one ever got anything out of my preaching, I had to accept the calling. But to God, it just didn't matter that I wasn't eloquent. It didn't matter to God that I wasn't a homiletical, hermeneutical, or philosophical type of person. To God, it only mattered that I loved Him, was willing to trust Him with my future, and cared about telling others about Him.

I share this with you because I want you to know that God will take care of you if you honor Him with your life. It took faith for me to leave the music industry. It took faith for me to leave the oil field and step out to fulfill the calling of ministry. But living for Jesus always takes faith! It always takes trust.

Sooner or later, we all have to trust God with our lives if we want to live out His plan for our lives. He can guide us and give us favor, but we've got to desire His help. We've got to desire Him. That means, knowing what His Word says and knowing Him as a friend must be important to us.

Now, during that time when I had just left the music industry and I was working for the trucking line selling pipe, nothing was more important to me than knowing more about God. I saturated myself with the things of God. I went to church every time the doors were open and absorbed what the preacher said. I spent a lot of time at night just reading my Bible, studying, going over the Scriptures I'd learned in church, and just reading on my own. I got a concordance and a Bible dictionary—I was serious about learning more about God!

I would listen to every preaching tape I could get my hands on. I listened to messages from all types of ministries and especially enjoyed messages from the faith ministries. They'd just stir me up! I heard about God's goodness, grace, and mercy. Then, I'd hear about what it meant to trust God and have strong faith in His Word. That was right up my alley. I knew what trusting God was about!

At that point in my life, I was interested in one thing and one thing only—hearing God's voice and knowing His plan for my life. I wanted to know God in a really intimate way. I knew He loved me, and I wanted Him to be my best friend. I'd think, *Best friends talk, right? Let's You and me talk, God!*

I read in the Bible where God showed Himself and audibly talked to Old Testament men like Adam, Noah, and Abraham, and I began to pray about God talking to me too.

When I prayed, I would reason with God by saying, "God, You showed yourself to Adam. You showed Yourself to Noah and Abraham too. You talked to all these people in my Bible and they got to see You. Why can't I see You too? Why can't I hear Your voice just like they did? Why can't You talk out loud to me? I want to see You, God! I want to see You!"

I wasn't praying right because I was a baby Christian and I didn't have a lot of sense! But my heart was seeking to know God more. I just wanted to touch Him, to feel Him, and to see Him with my own eyes. Now, God never promised that He would show Himself or talk audibly to anyone. In fact, it's better if you simply believe without seeing Him, because it is evidence that your faith is at work. But I was very interested in this, and in fact, during this time in my life, I was pretty belligerent about it! I was a baby Christian who had his diapers on and I was ready to see my Daddy!

I figured that if God would show Himself to people like Moses and Abraham, then there was no reason He wouldn't do the same for me. I had faith that He could, so I began to really seek Him in prayer and read through my Bible finding all the instances where God showed Himself or spoke directly to people, outside of the still, small voice.

There are so many supernatural events in the Bible that involved God personally talking to someone. It seems like God was looking for ways to talk to mankind! He wanted to talk to His kids. Anyone who would truly seek Him would find Him. He used all sorts of ways to get through to His children. These were the days before there was even a Bible.

I wanted to hear God so badly that it was on my heart day and night. God knew that I was seeking Him with my whole heart, and one day, while Cathy and I were attending a revival service, a preacher called me out of my seat and told me that he had a message from God for me. It was 1976.

I Was Granted a Visitation

He said, "You sir, come up here."

I said, "Me?" Because the first thing you think of when someone asks you to get out of your seat and go to the front of the church is, *Oh God, what did I do wrong? What did I do wrong? What did I do wrong?* And I thought to myself, *Well, I don't think I have done anything wrong.* But I wasn't too sure.

"Bring your wife up here with you," the preacher said. Cathy got up and walked up to the altar with me.

When we get to the front, the preacher says this:

"I don't know who you are, sir, but the Lord tells me that you have been asking to see Him."

When the man said that, my antenna went up! I was thinking, *Come on, my man! Tell me some more!*

He said, "The Lord told me to tell you He shall grant you a visitation."

I said to myself, *I have been praying two years and thought God hadn't heard a thing I'd said.*

The preacher continued, "He's coming to see you. He shall come to you at night. You shall be in bed with your wife. She will be sleeping. She will not hear and will not wake up. But the Lord will come to see you."

I asked, "When?"

The man said, "Quickly."

I was so excited. I went home and thought it would happen that very night. Cathy went to bed and I just waited up. I just knew that the preacher was a man of God and that God was going to visit me. So that night I did not sleep. I waited and waited and waited all night and He didn't come. It made me mad. The next day, I did the same thing, and again, He didn't come. I did this for three or four days in a row. No sleep. Just waiting on God.

About two weeks later, God still hadn't come over to my house! I got aggravated and I thought, *That guy missed it! God doesn't want to see me!*

Now, I was a baby Christian and I just wanted to do something for God, but I didn't know how to go about it. People always told me to do things for God, but they never told me how to do them. They told me to be healed. I'd say, "Okay, how?" They'd say, "Be blessed!" But

I'd think, *But how?* I didn't have a lot of teaching in that time of my life, and what practical messages I did hear were few and far between.

So about two weeks after the revival, I just decided to go to bed normally and not think about what the preacher said to me. Cathy went to bed first, like she usually did, while I stayed up and prayed a little while longer. This particular night, about two weeks after the revival, I prayed like I normally do, thanked God for the day, and then fell off to sleep.

Our bedroom was a small rectangular room with a door that entered on one of the long walls. If you walked through the door, you immediately saw the bed, and over the bed was a window with curtains. I slept on the left; Cathy slept on the right. I had an end table by the bed with my clock on it.

Now, I am a stomach sleeper and always have been. I never sleep on my back. I usually end up sleeping with my hands tucked under my pillow, and then I wake up because my hands start tingling when they fall asleep under the weight of my own head!

This night, I fell asleep as usual, but in the middle of the night, I suddenly woke up—for what I thought was no reason at all. My arms were still wrapped around my pillow and my head was facing the wall. I looked at the clock and it was 3:00 A.M. I just woke up and I didn't think anything about it, but I did notice that my hands weren't tingling from being under my pillow too long. Suddenly, I felt air blowing on me. It wasn't coming from the side where I was facing and it wasn't coming from Cathy's side, but it was blowing on my back from the end of the bed.

At first, I thought it was just the thermostat kicking on the air condition and blowing air through the vent. But suddenly, the wind got stronger. And then, stronger again. This wind was hitting my back with force and it began to go through my body.

As unbelievable as it seems, what I'm about to describe really happened and I had never felt anything like it before. This wind began to blow through my body. It blew out of my eyes, under my fingernails, and was coming out of the pores of my skin! When I tell you that it was blowing *through* me, I mean that it was blowing *through* me. It freaked me out! I stayed pinned to the bed with my eyes fixed on the clock. I didn't move an inch!

Suddenly, the wind picked up the curtains above our bed and threw them up the wall and over the top of the curtain rods. All of a sudden, I heard a voice.

"You asked to see Me. Turn around."

I was scared. I was nervous. I was amazed. Suddenly I knew that God was *big*. That may sound funny to you because it's so obvious, but you just don't realize the magnitude of God until His Spirit is in your room blowing up your curtains on their rods!

I stayed right where I was, looking at the clock.

The voice came again.

"You asked to see Me. Turn around."

Now, the wind was still blowing through my body, under my fingernails, and coming out of my pores. I was as physically awake as I am right now.

I said, "God!" I thought, *No. No. No. Back up, You are hurting me.*

The wind made me feel like my flesh was jumping off my bones. My skin was moving so hard under the force of that wind that I felt literal pain. Not excruciating pain, but my body could not handle it.

I thought to myself, *Cathy will look at Him. Cathy will do it!* So I moved against the wind a little and stretched out my elbow. I wouldn't pull my hands out from under my pillow! My face was still turned to the clock on the end table. The curtains were still flipping up against that wall on top of the rods. But I pushed my body towards the middle of the bed where Cathy was and jabbed her with my elbow.

The woman was sleeping like the dead! I nudged her, and I don't mean lightly! *Cathy, get up! Get up! Get up! Come on, get up!* I thought this to myself as I kept jabbing her with my elbow.

And there is Cathy, just sleeping away! She moaned a little and kept right on sleeping! I thought, *Man, Cathy! Don't you know God's in the room!*

A third time the voice came.

"You asked to see Me. Turn around."

"God," I answered, "forgive me for being so stupid. Forgive me. I prayed wrong." I knew that I wasn't going to turn around and look at Him. I knew Cathy wasn't going to wake up and that I just wasn't going to obey Him and turn around. I just couldn't do it. I don't know why. Now, I know I could have physically moved and looked. But it seemed that my fear kept me pinned to the bed. It was so intense, and I was completely out of breath from swinging so hard with my elbow jabbing Cathy, trying to get her to wake up.

Suddenly, the wind lessened. Then it completely stopped and the room was silent. When the room went quiet, I spun around and looked.

But nothing was there.

Then I got so angry with myself! Out loud I started talking to myself, "You stupid idiot! What is the matter with you? You asked to see God. Then when He comes to see you, you don't even turn around!"

I was so aggravated with myself. I looked over at Cathy and she was snoozing, so I jabbed her with my elbow again. And what do you know? The woman woke up!

Groggily she said, "What's the matter?"

"You just missed it!"

"What?"

"God was here in this very room, but you *had* to sleep! So just go on back to sleep!"

"What did He look like?" she asked.

"I... I... I didn't turn around!"

I was so aggravated, I got out of bed. And I was hungry, so I went to the refrigerator and made myself a sandwich. I went into my living room, plopped down on the couch, and started talking to God.

"God, You came to me. I heard You with my physical ears, and I didn't even turn around!"

And I heard His still, small voice in my spirit.

"I'm glad you didn't. It's better that you not see Me and still believe."

"But it's my heart's desire to see You."

"You wouldn't be able to handle My glory. You're living in a corruptible vessel, a body that will die."

"Is that why I was hurting?"

"That's why your flesh was hurting. Your flesh cannot handle the glory of Who I am."

I went back to eating my sandwich and then went to bed again. To tell you the truth, I was hoping He'd come again and give me another chance! But He didn't.

The next morning, Cathy showed me a bruise on her arm. She didn't know where it came from. It was in the exact place I'd been jabbing her! I told her about it and she forgave me. I should have known she wasn't going to wake up, since that's what the man of God told me, but I knew that even though she hadn't been asking to see God, she was brave enough to turn and look! Maybe that's why God didn't come to see her! It might have ripped the skin right off of her body, and I'd have a skinless wife today!

This experience was wild and I told my pastor, who didn't know what to think of it. He'd never heard of that happening before. So, I told a man who was older in the Lord than him, and he told me that I would be a preacher one day. I didn't want to be a preacher. I just wanted to be a good Christian and sit in the pew and learn.

I was too young in the Lord back then to become a preacher anyway, and I knew it. God doesn't send baby Christians into the five-fold ministry of pastor, teacher, prophet, apostle, or evangelist. That's His executive branch, and He doesn't fill it with babies!

I had a lot more growing up to do when it came to the things of God before I could hear and accept the calling I have today. I had to get more of the Word of God into my mind and my heart. I had to grow in understanding and digest more of what the Word said. Mainly, I had to grow in wisdom.

But God began to deal with me in special ways like this. And much of the time, I didn't tell anyone about it. I didn't want them to think I was a flake! I didn't want them to think I was some crazy person walking around!

I believe God came and visited me for a reason. He knew I wouldn't turn around. But He came anyway. It proved something to me that day. It proved that I didn't have to see God with my eyes to know that He exists. I didn't have to hear His voice with my own ears to know that He is alive.

I knew all of that in my heart before He ever came calling. That night proved to me that my faith was in God. I didn't doubt He could visit me and He did.

My faith hadn't ever come from experiences. It came from my saturation of the Word of God. Romans 10:17 says, *"So then faith cometh by hearing, and hearing by the word of God."* I had developed my faith by reading and hearing the Word, meditating on the Word, and studying the Word of God to such a point that I literally believed that God would, in fact, visit me. And He did. He honored me; He didn't have to, but He did.

Today I know what the audible voice of God sounds like! And, man, it's *big!*

CHAPTER 7

The "Always Available" Holy-Spirit

God has always been trying to get through to His kids. If you read through the Old Testament, you'll find some interesting and often odd methods of communication between God and His people! Sometimes God picked certain men who loved Him and sought to do right, and spoke directly to them about their lives, the lives of their family, and even the whole nation. He would speak through dreams, visions, an audible voice, and all sorts of different ways!

There were major prophets back in the Old Testament who heard the voice of God over and over again. They heard what God said. It was written down, and today we have some of the spoken Word of God on paper in the form of our Holy Bible! That's one of the reasons we call the Bible God's *Word*.

At one time God talked to a whole nation of Israel, but they didn't like hearing His voice. It scared them, and so they said, "Don't talk to us! Talk to Moses, and then he'll relay what you say." God honored their request and from then on spoke only to individuals who sought

Him out. Only those who loved God and sought after God's heart would be anointed to hear His voice and/or know His plan.

It is interesting to study the experiences of some of those anointed men who clearly heard from God, such as:

Joseph	(Genesis 41:38)
Moses	(Numbers 11:17)
Joshua	(Numbers 27:18)
Gideon	(Judges 6:34)
Samson	(Judges 14:6-19, 15:14,15)
Saul	(1 Samuel 10:10, 11:6)
David	(1 Samuel 16:13)
Elijah	(1 Kings 18:12; 2 Kings 2:16)
Elisha	(2 Kings 2:15)
Zechariah	(2 Chronicles 24:20)
Ezekiel	(Ezekiel 2:2)
Daniel	(Daniel 4:9)
Micah	(Micah 3:8)

All these Old Testament men were anointed by the Holy Spirit to hear God's voice. Some heard about His plan for their life. Others heard God's plan for the lives of others. But God didn't exclusively speak to prophets. He would talk to anyone who really sought to know Him.

There were a lot of people who wanted to know *about* God, but not as many who really wanted to *know* God. For those who sought after God, even before the blood of Jesus broke down the wall of sin, God would send His Holy Spirit to rest on people and anoint them to hear His voice.

The Holy Spirit has always had a role in speaking God's will to His people. Although the Holy Spirit worked on the earth and spoke to men who sought after God, I believe His greatest work didn't really come until after Jesus died and went to Heaven! Now, that's when things changed for the Holy Spirit.

After Jesus paid the price for the world's sin through His sinless life and innocent death, the barrier that stood between God and man fell down, and suddenly God's Holy Spirit got a new job! He was able to actually inhabit those who accepted Jesus' sacrifice and fill them up with God's holy presence! This sounds strange to the natural mind, but it is the miracle of being "born again." The Holy Spirit could then literally come and dwell within every believer. This is the great and wonderful work of the cross.

To have the Holy Spirit living within a person was unheard of before Jesus died, rose again, and went to Heaven. But He warned His-disciples that it was going to happen. I'll get more into that in chapter eight!

Jesus Loved His Disciples

You've got to understand something about Jesus. He flat loved His disciples. He cared about them so much that He told them the plan of redemption before He went to the cross. He also told them what He would do for them after He died and went back home to Heaven. To Jesus, these guys were not just a bunch of staff members. He had a personal relationship with all of them. Jesus wasn't a fly-by-night preacher who left His staff high and dry once He went on to Heaven. The fact that He made them a promise that He'd send Someone to them once He'd left showed how much He cared about them.

When Jesus left this earth, He wanted to make sure that His boys-knew that they wouldn't be left alone. He knew the stuff that they would have to deal with in life. He knew what we all would have-to deal with in life once He went home to His Father. Jesus knew-that His disciples, and everyone who followed after them, would need somebody to talk to, to comfort them, and to guide them in life. In fact, one day Jesus had a meeting with His staff to tell them all about it.

Jesus knew He was about to go to the cross. He knew that His boys were going to have to see Him beaten and bruised beyond recognition. They were going to see Him carry His cross up the long road to Calvary. They were going to see the nails go through His hands and feet, watch Him lifted up on that wooden cross, and see Him bleed for the sins of the world.

Now, it was going to be rough for Jesus' disciples to see that, and He knew it. But when He took a look around at His boys, He knew they wouldn't be able to take it without Him talking to them. So He said to Himself, "I've gotta let these boys know what's about to go down." Jesus didn't want them left without hope, wondering where He'd gone or what He was doing.

So He had a meeting with them to tell them about the next One He was going to get His Dad to send to the earth.

Jesus Meets with His Staff

Jesus knew how His boys could be! He knew that they'd be so disturbed in their hearts when He went to the cross that they wouldn't know what to do with themselves. So He spoke words that were not only meant for the disciples, but for everyone who would follow Christ after them.

In John 14 Jesus immediately starts warning them about how they were going to feel after His crucifixion:

"Let not your heart be troubled: ye believe in God, believe also in-me.

"In my Father's house are many mansions: if it were not so, I would have told you. I go to prepare a place for you.

"And if I go and prepare a place for you, I will come again, and receive you unto myself; that where I am, there ye may be also.

"And whither I go ye know, and the way ye know."

John 14:1-4

In other words, Jesus was saying, "Look, I'm about to bite the dust. But don't get down in the dumps when you see it happen. If you believe God, believe Me and what I'm about to tell you. I'm going to a good place. There are lots of nice houses where my Dad lives and I'm going back there to set you up with one of your own. So if I'm going to build you a house, don't you think I'm coming back for you? I'm coming back so that we can be together again."

This is a real comfort to us today, because no matter how bad life seems, we can be assured that Jesus has not left us or forgotten about us. He's in Heaven preparing a place for us and is coming back for us!-Not only that, but He's also about to send someone to help us day-to-day too. But I don't want to get ahead of myself, so let's go on to the story!

After Jesus said this, Thomas spoke up and said,

"Lord, we know not whither thou goest; and how can we know the way?

WANTING A GOD YOU CAN TALK TO

"Jesus saith unto him, I am the way, the truth, and the life: no man cometh unto the Father, but by me.

"If ye had known me, ye should have known my Father also: and from henceforth ye know him, and have seen him."

John 14:5-7

I'll paraphrase Jesus' words again, "Look, Thomas. I am the way to Heaven; you're looking at the *only* truth, and you're looking at the *only* way to eternal life. Nobody's getting to God unless they go through Me first. If you know Me, you know My Father, God. So you've known God and have seen Him with your own eyes just by looking at Me."

That's another comforting statement for those of us who know Jesus as personal Lord and Savior. Because of Jesus, we're in touch with Jehovah God! That's what salvation and communicating with God is all about.

Then Philip speaks up with a stupid request he wouldn't have even asked if he'd been listening to Jesus.

"Philip saith unto him, Lord, shew us the Father, and it sufficeth us" (John 14:8).

Jesus seems a little exasperated by this. He had just told them that if they saw Him then they'd seen the Father, but Philip must have missed that part of the conversation. Or, he just didn't grasp what Jesus was saying. Because to say, "Show us God and it will satisfy us" was a pretty dumb thing to say after what Jesus had just told them! You can tell Jesus is a little weary with this by what He says in response.

"Jesus saith unto him, Have I been so long time with you, and yet hast thou not known me, Philip? he that hath seen me

hath seen the Father; and how sayest thou then, Shew us the Father?"

John 14:9

In other words, "How long have I been with you, Philip? And you *still* don't know Who I am? I just told you that if you see Me, you see My Dad. We're one! How then can you say, 'Show me your Dad and it'll be enough?' " Then Jesus continues,

> *"Believest thou not that I am in the Father, and the Father in me? the words that I speak unto you I speak not of myself: but the Father that dwelleth in me, he doeth the works.*
>
> *"Believe me that I am in the Father, and the Father in me: or else believe me for the very works' sake.*
>
> *"Verily, verily, I say unto you, He that believeth on me, the works that I do shall he do also; and greater works than these shall he do; because I go unto my Father. And whatsoever ye shall ask in my name, that will I do, that the Father may be glorified in the Son. If ye shall ask any thing in my name, I will do it."*

John 14:10-14

Jesus is saying, "I'm not talking on My own here! God is talking through Me. He is doing the miracles. At least believe Me for the work that you've seen Me do. Believe in Me and you'll do even greater miracles than I've done. I'm going home to My Father, and when you have needs, if you ask God for things in My name, it'll happen. Anything you ask in My name when I'm gone, I'll do it!"

Jesus goes on to instruct them to act on what He's been teaching them saying, *"If ye love me, keep my commandments"* (John 14:15).

<hr>

Not Just Lip Service

Whew! Jesus brought it all down to love when He said, "Do you love Me, boys? Then do what I say." Love is the key. Do you love Jesus? Then do what He said. Jesus told His disciples that after He went to the cross and died, He would pray to the Father for the Holy Spirit to help believers out.

The bottom line is that you are saved by grace because that's the only way anybody can be saved. Salvation sure doesn't just happen because you do a few good deeds. Good deeds are wonderful, but you can't ever be better than the blood of Jesus. That's all God accepts if you want to talk to Him. It was a precious thing for God to send His only Son to shed innocent blood for us.

But after we accept His sacrifice and are righteous before God, it's time to do something about it! In other words, it's not just about lip service; it's about service! We are saved by grace, but after that, we have to do what Jesus said if we really love Him. Works still matter in that respect.

There are real extremes of teaching regarding both grace and works. Some people say it's only what you do (works) that counts. Others say it doesn't matter what you do because God's grace is enough. Both are right but they're not talking about the same thing! Grace is for salvation and for removing sin. But God never meant for us to lie on our backsides and do nothing, knowing that we're on our way to Heaven. There is a lost and dying world of people out there.

How Grace and Works Go Together

When I was a kid, I started out going to churches that were extreme on the grace message—extreme meaning that it didn't matter what I did as long as I came back to church and told the leader about it. Nobody seemed to expect much out of you. It's as if they figured that everybody was so bad that they had to make some concessions and not preach too hard against anything.

Most of these people I went to church with were nice and sweet, but they couldn't have cared less about doing anything for God. They didn't crack open a Bible or even think about Jesus all week long. Sunday was a social ritual, a place you checked out people's new clothes and didn't feel pressured to really change anything about yourself. It didn't matter if you went to church or not, because basically, you stayed the same anyway.

I went to other churches that were extreme on works—extreme meaning that it didn't seem to matter where your heart was, as long as you were doing good deeds or lots of stuff for the church. Some of the people I went to church with were so bitter and mean, but they were there every time the church doors were open and felt righteous for it. Church was a legalistic, rule-pushing bunch of grumpy people who never looked happy but always did good deeds.

These were the kind of people who would walk up to you on the street with a sad, disgusted look on their face and say in a nasal, whiny tone of voice, "Would you like to meet Jesus as the Lord of your life?" You'd take one look at them and think to yourself, *Whatever you've got, I don't want it! It looks painful!*

When you grow up around extremism like that, it just pushes you away from God. Kids see hypocrisy so easily, and it affects the way they think about God. That's what happened to me, and it took years before I would even consider turning to God. Today I know that you just can't accept God's grace and keep on sinning, because if you do, you don't love Jesus. Hey, I didn't say it! Don't get mad at me! It was Jesus Who said, *"If ye love me, keep my commandments."*

And now I know that you can't leave your heart any old way you want to and get to Heaven based on how many good deeds you do. That's called frustrating the grace of God!

Frustrating Grace

Galatians 2:21 says, *"I do not frustrate the grace of God: for if righteousness come by the law, then Christ is dead in vain."* The law was basically the Jewish rulebook. So in other words, this passage is saying, "Jesus didn't die for nothing! You can't gain righteousness and get close to God by only what you do!"

Put that up against most of Jesus' teachings in the Gospels of Matthew, Mark, Luke, and John, and you'll see that Jesus was very interested in what His followers did. Adhering to the commandments was important to Jesus, and He often went a step further in His encouragement to His followers to lead holy and blameless lives. But Jesus didn't mean for our lives to be tough, where we're always trying to grasp the brass ring and never quite making it.

Jesus wanted us to understand that He loves us, that the Father is available through Him. And that once we accept Him, God will accept us. And once that happens, well, the sky's the limit! Because of Jesus, our heart changes. When the heart of a person changes, their works just naturally start changing too. It's not a tough "trying to attain" mentality. It's a natural progression; after salvation you just start wanting to do the right thing!

So grace and works are entirely separate when it comes to salvation, and you can only be saved by grace, which simply means that God accepts Jesus' shed blood for your past, present, and future sins. But after you accept that grace, you're to begin a life of good works.

Now, don't think that after you get saved, grace stops working! Because it doesn't! That's what some churches teach when they lead you to believe that every bad thing you do can put you in Hell, and every good thing you do can put you in Heaven! You'd be in and out of Hell so much, you wouldn't know what to do with yourself!

After you're saved, you still receive God's grace continually. If you mess up, God's grace is there with the blood of Jesus to erase the sin. All you have to do is ask for forgiveness and it's gone. You move on in life and don't beat yourself over the head about it. That guilt stuff is not from God. Once you say, "God, I'm sorry, please forgive me" you should accept that Jesus' blood is good enough to wash that sin away and not keep feeling guilty. Just make a point not to do it again. Pray to God about helping you out in that area.

That day, Jesus was talking to His disciples and said, "If you love Me, do My commandments." But Jesus wasn't finished talking in this passage of John chapter fourteen! Now, let's move off of this part of the verse and on to the next, because this is where it really gets good.

Next, Jesus tells His disciples about "another" Comforter and the wonderful day the Power came!

CHAPTER 8

The Day the Power Came

Then Jesus said, *"And I will pray the Father, and he shall give you **another Comforter**, that he may abide with you for ever"* (John-14:16).

In that very important passage of Scripture, Jesus promised to send *another* Comforter. Jesus was the disciples' Comforter while He was on the earth. He was the One Who helped them, soothed them in times of distress, relieved their minds when they had heavy life-burdens, and encouraged them day by day.

Now, Jesus was about to leave the earth, and He didn't want to leave them comfortless. He promised that although He had to do the work of redemption, which included death, He wouldn't leave them all alone to fend for themselves. He was going to send Someone to be their Comforter. Just like He did when He was on the earth, Jesus would send that Comforter to soothe them in times of distress, to relieve their minds when life gave them heavy burdens, to encourage them day by day, and to help them in times of need.

Jesus continued, *"Even the **Spirit of truth;** whom the world cannot receive, because it seeth him not, neither knoweth him:*

but ye-know him; for he dwelleth with you, and shall be in you"
(John-14:17).

Just before this, Jesus was calling the One He was going to pray
that His Dad will send to earth the name "Comforter." Now, Jesus is
calling this Comforter another name: the "Spirit of Truth."

He was also saying that people who didn't believe He was the
Son of God wouldn't be able to receive the Comforter/Spirit of Truth
that He was going to send. Jesus was reiterating His role as God's
mediator in that verse. To us, this simply means that a person can't be
filled with the Holy Spirit unless they accept Jesus. The Holy Spirit
may be around them, convicting their hearts of sin, but He won't
move into them and dwell within them until they say, "Jesus come
into my life..." and do what Romans 10:9,10 say to do!

Remember that the miracle of salvation is God's Spirit coming to
live in unity with your spirit. That is what re-creates you on the inside
and gives you that heart-change that begins to become a life-change.

Now, in John 14:18-20, Jesus says, ***"I will not leave you
comfortless: I will come to you.*** *Yet a little while, and the world seeth
me no more; but ye see me: because I live, ye shall live also. At that
day ye shall know that I am in my Father, and ye in me, and I in you."*

Jesus is talking about His death and how He was going to show
Himself supernaturally to the disciples afterward so they'd know He
was alive. And because they'd see Him alive, they'd know that they
would live on after death too.

> *"He that hath my commandments, and keepeth them, he it
> is that loveth me: and he that loveth me shall be loved of my
> Father, and I will love him, and will manifest myself to him."*
>
> John 14:21

Jesus was promising that those who loved Him enough to keep His commandments would also be loved by His Father. He said something odd though, right afterwards, about God manifesting Himself to them, and Judas interrupted Jesus' speech to question Him about it.

> *"Judas saith unto him, not Iscariot, Lord, how is it that thou wilt manifest thyself unto us, and not unto the world?*
>
> *"Jesus answered and said unto him, If a man love me, he will keep my words: and my Father will love him, and **we will come unto him, and make our abode with him.**"*

John 14:22,23

Jesus was talking about moving in and making an abode, or home, in them! He was talking about the indwelling of the Holy Spirit that was going to take place not long after His death for those who loved Him and kept His commandments.

> *"He that loveth me not keepeth not my sayings: and the-word which ye hear is not mine, but the Father's which sent me.*
>
> *"These things have I spoken unto you, being yet present with you.*
>
> ***"But the Comforter, which is the Holy Ghost, whom the Father will send in my name, he shall teach you all things, and bring all things to your remembrance, whatsoever I have said unto you.**"*

John 14:24-26

Jesus Still Preached after His Death

In Jesus' meeting with His staff, we learned that He was going to die, rise again, come back, talk with His disciples, and then ascend into Heaven where He would pray to His Dad to send the Holy Spirit. And the Holy Spirit would then come down and make His abode in the hearts of believers.

Guess what?

Jesus made good on His promise!

He did everything He said He would do. You can read about the amazing day the power of the Holy Spirit touched Jesus' followers in the Upper Room in Acts 2.

After Jesus died, He rose from the dead and then visited with His disciples again to teach them! Luke, Jesus' disciple, writes this to his friend Theo:

"The former treatise have I made, O Theophilus, of all that Jesus began both to do and teach,

"Until the day in which he was taken up, after that he through the Holy Ghost had given commandments unto the apostles whom he had chosen:

"To whom also He shewed himself alive after his passion by many infallible proofs, being seen of them forty days, and speaking of the things pertaining to the kingdom of God:

"And, being assembled together with them, commanded them that they should not depart from Jerusalem, but wait for the promise of the Father, which, saith he, ye have heard of me.

"For John truly baptized with water; but ye shall be baptized with the Holy Ghost not many days hence.

"When they therefore were come together, they asked of him, saying, Lord, wilt thou at this time restore again the kingdom to Israel?

"And he said unto them, It is not for you to know the times or the seasons, which the Father hath put in his own power.

"But ye shall receive power, after that the Holy Ghost is come upon you: and ye shall be witnesses unto me both in Jerusalem, and in all Judaea, and in Samaria, and unto the uttermost part of the earth.

"And when he had spoken these things, while they beheld,-he was taken up; and a cloud received him out of their sight."

Acts 1:1-9

After His crucifixion, death, and resurrection, Jesus hung out for forty days talking to His followers! He told them that they'd be baptized with the Holy Ghost not too many days in the future and that the baptism would give them power to be witnesses for Him.

Not long after He ascended into Heaven, when the disciples were assembled in a place called the Upper Room, something wild happened. You may have heard people say that the Holy Spirit came on the Day of Pentecost.

The Day the Power Came

Pentecost was a yearly festival for the Jewish people where the men went to Jerusalem to celebrate the first buds of their crop harvest. On this particular festival day, many of Jesus' followers were assembled in a place in Jerusalem the Scripture calls the Upper Room. The Bible tells the story in Acts 2:1,2.

"And when the day of Pentecost was fully come, they were all with one accord in one place.

"And suddenly there came a sound from heaven as of a rushing mighty wind, and it filled all the house where they were sitting."

I know what the wind of God's presence feels like, and it is powerful! This was a supernatural thing that was happening. Verses three and four tell what happens next!

*"And there appeared unto them **cloven tongues like as of fire, and it sat upon each of them.***

"And they were all filled with the Holy Ghost, and began to speak with other tongues, as the Spirit gave them utterance."

This is where the phenomenon of speaking in tongues began! It began when the Power of God came down in the form of the Holy Ghost and baptized everyone in the room! This day, the Holy Spirit made His entry into the hearts of believers, and it was the real beginning of the New Testament church.

In fact, the story is in the book of Acts for a reason. What you'll read in that book are the "acts" of the apostles, not just the teachings. The Holy Spirit is the active member of the Trinity, so it would only stand to reason that He'd make His presence known so dramatically in the book of Acts.

In the book of Acts, there are five different accounts of people receiving the Holy Spirit and speaking in other tongues. (Acts 2:4; Acts 8:14-25; Acts 9:17-20; Acts 10:44-48 and Acts 19:1-7.)

The Power to Witness to Everyone

During the first mass baptism in Acts 2, the people spoke in "other tongues." This meant that, although there were people from all the Jewish nations present for the annual festival of Pentecost who spoke many different languages, when the followers of Jesus were baptized and began to speak, they spoke in a language that *everyone who heard them was able to understand*. They didn't understand what they were saying, but to the hearers it was as if the *followers of Jesus were speaking their own language*. This gave them the ability to witness to everyone.

It was a miraculous day.

God wanted to talk, to let all those people know about His Son. So He was supernaturally dropping words on the tongues of Jesus' followers, making them able to be understood by everyone as they witnessed for Christ.

We Aren't Drunk

Acts 2:5-12 tells how some of the people responded to this great miracle.

"And there were dwelling at Jerusalem Jews, devout men, out of every nation under heaven.

"Now when this was noised abroad, the multitude came together, and were confounded, because that every man heard them speak in his own language.

"And they were all amazed and marveled, saying one to another, Behold, are not all these which speak Galilaeans?

"And how hear we every man in our own tongue, wherein we were born?

"Parthians, and Medes, and Elamites, and the dwellers in Mesopotamia, and in Judaea, and Cappadocia, in Pontus, and Asia,

"Phrygia, and Pamphylia, in Egypt, and in the parts of Libya about Cyrene, and strangers of Rome, Jews and proselytes,

"Cretes and Arabians, we do hear them speak in our tongues the wonderful works of God.

"And they were all amazed, and were in doubt, saying one to another, **What meaneth this?"**

Now, some people mocked tongues and said, "They are full of new wine!" But when Peter heard this, he stood up with the other disciples and said:

"Ye men of Judaea, and all ye that dwell at Jerusalem, be this known unto you, and hearken to my words:

"For these are not drunken, as ye suppose, seeing it is but the third hour of the day.

"But this is that which was spoken by the prophet Joel;

"And it shall come to pass in the last days, saith God, I will pour out of my Spirit upon all flesh: and your sons and your daughters shall prophesy, and your young men shall see visions, and your old men shall dream dreams:

"And on my servants and on my handmaidens I will pour out in those days of my Spirit; and they shall prophesy:

"And I will shew wonders in heaven above, and signs in the earth beneath; blood, and fire, and vapor of smoke:

"The sun shall be turned into darkness, and the moon into blood, before that great and notable day of the Lord come:

"And it shall come to pass, that whosoever shall call on the name of the Lord shall be saved."

Acts 2:14-21

Peter's First Holy Ghost Sermon

Peter told all the people about Jesus and how He'd been crucified and was now in Heaven seated on the throne. The people's hearts were open to hear the message. And do you know what the message was?

"Repent, and be baptized every one of you in the name of Jesus Christ for the remission of sins, and ye shall receive the gift of the Holy Ghost.

"For the promise is unto you, and to your children, and to all that are afar off, even as many as the Lord our God shall call."

Acts 2:38,39

This Scripture lets us know that the promise of the baptism of the Holy Ghost was not just for those who were there to hear the message, but also for their children and to all those who lived far away, as many as the Lord would call. Call to what? Call to salvation! Then Peter testified and exhorted the people with more Holy Ghost preaching. Guess what happened next?

> *"Then Peter said unto them, Repent, and be baptized every one of you in the name of Jesus Christ for the remission of sins, and ye shall receive the gift of the Holy Ghost."*
>
> Acts 2:38

The boy gave an altar call! Three thousand people came forward to get saved, get water baptized, and receive the baptism of the Holy Ghost that day!

> *"Then they that gladly received his word were baptized: and the same day there were added unto them about three thousand souls."*
>
> Acts 2:41

That amazing Day of Pentecost began the tongue-talking church that we have today. While this amazing phenomenon began with tongues being spoken and people understanding it in their own language, the apostle Paul also describes another kind of tongue in 1-Corinthians 13:1, the tongue of angels.

Some people call this the unknown tongue, when you are given a holy language of God through the baptism of the Holy Spirit and no one understands it but God. The apostle Paul says, "Though I speak with the tongues of men and *of angels...*."

We Have the Same Spirit Today

This fire of the Holy Ghost that inhabited the men and women on the Day of Pentecost over two thousand years ago is the same Holy Spirit Who is still on earth today.

Why is He still here? To continue doing the same thing He did back then! To give us boldness to witness for Christ so that the whole earth can hear about God's plan for man! And to comfort, guide, and bless us by speaking to our hearts the messages of God.

That's the power of the Holy Ghost!

CHAPTER 9

The Still, Small Voice

As powerful as tongues were on the Day of Pentecost and as great as it is to be able to pray *"...in the tongues of men and of angels,"* it doesn't take the place of other ways God talks to and through His people.

If you're born again, you can hear God's voice. The Holy Spirit is God's voice within the earth. But whether you have experienced the baptism of the Holy Spirit and spoken in tongues or not, you can hear God's voice. You can hear His voice a minute after you accept Jesus as your Savior, because once you're born again, the Holy Spirit comes to live within you.

God is that close to you!

The only requirement to hearing His voice is accepting His Son and loving Him enough to obey His commandments. But the question is, are you listening on a spiritual level or on a mental level? There are many ways God speaks to His kids, but most of the time He does it through the still, small voice you hear coming from your heart when you're praying.

The words "still, small voice" come from an Old Testament story about Elijah in 1 Kings 19:1-12. In this passage, the prophet Elijah is running from Jezebel. She wants him dead and promises him that death is coming soon. He runs out to the wilderness to hide. He's sitting out there under a juniper tree, feeling miserable and hungry, and just begging God to take him home to Heaven. He falls asleep under that tree because he's exhausted and stressed out.

Then God sends an angel to bake him some bread and bring him some water. The angel says, "Arise and eat." He wakes up and sees a jar of water and a cake of bread right by his head. Elijah eats and drinks some and then goes back to sleep!

Then the angel comes a second time and touches Elijah, and tells him to wake up and eat some more because the journey ahead is going to be too hard if he doesn't.

Elijah doesn't eat again for forty days because that angel's food sustains him as he journeys to Mount Horeb. Elijah is hanging out in a cave when God starts talking to him:

"And he came thither unto a cave, and lodged there; and, behold, the word of the LORD came to him, and he said unto him, What doest thou here, Elijah?

"And he said, I have been very jealous for the LORD God of hosts: for the children of Israel have forsaken thy covenant, thrown down thine altars, and slain thy prophets with the sword; and I, even I only, am left; and they seek my life, to take it away.

"And he said, Go forth, and stand upon the mount before the LORD. And, behold, the LORD passed by, and a great and strong wind rent the mountains, and brake in pieces the rocks before the LORD; but the LORD was not in the wind:

and after the wind an earthquake; but the LORD was not in the earthquake:

*"And after the earthquake a fire; but the LORD was not in the fire: and after the fire **a still small voice.**"*

1 Kings 19:9-12

What I want you to notice about this passage is that even though there were dramatic things going on, God's voice wasn't in them. There was a wind that was so strong it busted up the rocks on the mountain! There was an earthquake and lastly, a fire.

But God wasn't in any of those things.

After the fire is when He spoke up, and He didn't use a thundering, loud voice.

Instead, God chose a *still, small voice.*

When Elijah heard this, he wrapped his face in his cloth mantle and stood in the entrance of the cave to hear the still, small voice of God.

Heart and Spirit

That same still, small voice comes into our hearts when we get saved. The Holy Spirit lives within us, and it is His voice that communicates with us.

When people talk about hearing God's voice, they will often interchange the words *heart* and *spirit.* Even though we know God's Spirit communicates with our spirit, people will say that God spoke something to their "heart" because the still, small voice seems to come from the heart area of the body. Most people understand what you're saying when you interchange the two words.

James 4:8 begins by saying, *"Draw nigh to God, and he will draw nigh to you."* So there's a commitment on God's part that if you get close to Him, He'll get close to you. But there is also a commandment there to clean yourself up (by asking for forgiveness for any sin you might have done), and don't be wish-washy.

James 4:8 ends by saying, *"...Cleanse your hands, ye sinners; and purify your hearts, ye double minded."* You have the ability to choose what you will believe. That's God's gift of free will in action. But going back and forth between what you believe just makes you more and more confused.

If one day you think God talks to you and the next day you don't, you're being double-minded. If you're having a hard time hearing God's voice, make a decision to believe by faith that God talks to His kids. Say to yourself, "I believe that God spoke to people in the Bible, and He talks to people every day. I know His Holy Spirit lives in me and He will speak to my heart too."

Your old, pre-saved mentality may tell you one thing and the Bible may tell you another. Go with what the Bible says and don't switch back and forth between the two mind-sets. Accept that if God's Word says it, then it must be true, regardless of what anybody says about it. That's what I do and it works. I know what I believe. It's called the Bible. I don't flip-flop on God's Word; I just believe it, accept it, and have faith in it. So it works for me. And if it works for me, it'll work for you.

I always say that you can't really be a good Christian until you lose your mind. I don't mean mental or emotional instability, because that never did anybody any good! What I mean is that you've got to lose that old, unsaved way of thinking if you want to understand the things of God. Your faith grows when you hear the Scriptures. Your spirit seems to get louder too! The more you get into God and His Word, the more He seems to get into you.

God likes to talk. Sometimes we just have to tune out the static that's cluttering our minds, tune in to His voice, and be quiet once in a while!

Give God Some Room

Now, this is a big problem I see as I travel preaching the Gospel. People complain about not hearing God's voice, but they're the ones who are always talking. They don't let God get a word in edgewise. They've been taught so much in the church about praying to God, but nobody told them to actually listen to God.

This is a tip that seems obvious, but I'm going to tell it to you anyway. After you pray, be quiet for a bit. Pray and think about something in the Word of God. Then give God some room to say something to you.

Some people say, "Oh, Lord, Lord, please help me, Lord! Please help meeeee! Oh, Lord, I need help, I need help, I need help! I need help right now, Lord, Jesus, right now...."

God's probably up there trying to squeeze something in like, "Psst...hey...yeah...." He's a gentleman though, so He won't barge right in and talk over you.

People always ask me why I'm so happy. Well, for one, I'm not dying and going to Hell! Number two, the Bible is a good book that gives you practical ways to live a good life. And number three, I have God living on the inside of me, and that means I'm never alone! I have someone to talk to!

I've decided to live my life this way because it's a better life to be in communication with God. It makes me happy. I'm happy because I have Jesus here with me through the miracle of the new birth. He's not an absent Jesus! He's right here with me, and having a Bible is like having a training manual for daily living.

The Spirit of Truth

In John 15:26 Jesus said, *"But when the Comforter is come, whom I will send unto you from the Father, even the **Spirit of truth**, which proceedeth from the Father, he shall testify of Me...."*

That word "testify" comes from the word *martureo*, and according to the *Strong's Exhaustive Concordance*, it means "to be witness, i.e. testify (literally or figuratively)." In the King James Version it means to "charge, give [evidence], bear record, have (obtain, of) good (honest) report, be well reported of, testify, give (have) testimony, (be, bear, give, obtain) witness."

So when we're talking about hearing God's voice, this Scripture is important because it means that when you're talking to the Holy Spirit, you're going to hear the truth. You're also going to hear about the importance of Jesus and His teachings.

The Holy Spirit *speaks* truth.

Jesus is truth.

When the Voice Isn't God

If you're hearing a voice coming into your head and it is saying something other than the truth of Jesus Christ, you are not talking to the Holy Spirit! That's a lying spirit, and you know where it comes from! Send it back to where it came from by rebuking it in the name of Jesus and say, "I will not listen to any lying spirit of the devil." Then resist it and it will leave. Don't play with it. Don't talk to it. Resist it and it will leave. That's what you're supposed to do according to the Bible.

"Submit yourselves therefore to God. Resist the devil, and he will flee from you" (James 4:7). Submit yourself to God, and don't submit yourself to other lying voices that would tell you something other than what is in the Holy Word of God. Resist and the devil will flee from you. Don't be a double-minded person by entertaining some lying thought. Instead, draw near to God and He'll draw near to you.

Remember that God doesn't argue with Himself. You never hear about Jesus, God, and the Holy Spirit arguing in the Bible. God never says, "Jesus, shut up and sit down!" Jesus never said once in the Bible, "God, that's a dumb idea and I am not going to do it." The Holy Spirit never said, "I'm tired of filling these people up with You, God! I'm tired of having to wait for them to talk to Jesus first. Why can't I do things my own way for once?"

That may sound funny to you, but God isn't confused. God is not a schizophrenic. He doesn't talk out of both sides of His mouth. There are no church splits in God's Holy Trinity.

Testing the Spirit

In 1 John 4:1-4, there is a Scripture that tells us what to do when we are unsure if what we're hearing is from the Spirit of God.

"Beloved, believe not every spirit, but try the spirits whether they are of God: because many false prophets are gone out into the world" (v. 1).

So, you're supposed to test the spirit if you think it's not from God. How do you do that?

"Hereby know ye the Spirit of God: Every spirit that confesseth that Jesus Christ is come in the flesh is of God" (v-2).

So you know that it is the Spirit of God if it confesses that Jesus was God in the flesh.

"And every spirit that confesseth not that Jesus Christ is come in the flesh is not of God: and this is that spirit of antichrist, whereof ye have heard that it should come; and even now already is it in the world" (v. 3).

And because of this Scripture, you know that if the spirit does not confess that Jesus was God in the flesh, then it's an "anti" Christ spirit—and that just means that it's against God.

"Ye are of God, little children, and have overcome them: because greater is he that is in you, than he that is in the world" (v. 4).

This Scripture encourages you to not worry about lying spirits, because they're not more powerful than you! God is living in you! What can a stupid lying devil do when you've got God's Holy Spirit living in you? Nothing! Nothing except what you'll let him do. You're-more powerful because God is greater than any other spirit in this world.

God Won't Go Against His Word

John 16:13 reminds us again that when the Spirit of Truth comes upon the scene, He will only *"...guide you into all truth: for He shall not speak of Himself; but whatsoever He shall hear, that shall He speak: and He will shew you things to come."*

The reality is that God spelled out His will in His Word. Sometimes I hear people say things that they believe God told them in their spirit, but it goes directly against His Word. That's why we need to read, understand, and digest the Word of God in our lives. It helps us to distinguish God's voice from our own voice or even a lying devil's voice.

You know that you're hearing your own voice or the devil's voice when you hear words that aren't biblical. Sometimes I see this when I travel. I'll meet people who don't read the Word of God or study to understand it, and then they try to say God told them something that goes directly against the Bible. I can't count how many times I've heard people tell me that God said something that I know that He wouldn't have said!

I've heard people say things like, "You know, Brother Jesse, God told me to quit my job, leave my wife and children, and just follow Him. Wherever He tells me to go, that's where I'm going to go. I know that God will take care of the wife and kids. I've got to do what He told me to do. And I have such a peace about it, Brother Jesse, I really do."

They think they sound spiritual but I'm thinking, *That's nuts!* Did God say, "Abandon thy children" in His Word? No! He said, *"But if any provide not for his own, and specially for those of his own house, he hath denied the faith, and is worse than an infidel"* (1-Timothy 5:8). Worse than an infidel sounds pretty bad to me! It doesn't sound like God agrees with men who abandon their kids and don't financially provide for their family.

If God tells you to go do some work for Him and you must leave your family for a time, He will never tell you to leave them without financial support. You must support your family or you've "denied the faith," and God says you're "worse than an infidel."

If a man can't work, that's one thing. But I've heard of men not wanting to work just so they can stay home and read the Word. If a man is lying around the house while his kids starve because God told him to stay home and read the Bible all day, well, he's living in a dream world! God didn't tell any man to do that, ever! God is honorable, and He doesn't encourage anyone to shuck his responsibilities. They might have "a peace about it," but if it goes against the Word of God, it's a false peace, and soon enough they will have a serious lack of peace!

When people tell me God told them to leave their spouse, take something that doesn't belong to them, or dishonor someone else, I know that they aren't hearing from God. God won't go against His Word! Some people just have no wisdom when it comes to this.

"But God Told Me to Do This!"

You'll hear a misguided believer say, "God told me to do this," and it's totally against His Word and His nature. They may steal money from the church and say, "God told me to take this because the church is really just the people of God in general and I really need a new microwave." No, God wouldn't tell anybody to steal money from anybody else. He wouldn't tell you to steal your neighbor's lawn furniture because all things belong to Him! He wouldn't tell you to pocket a five-dollar bill as the offering plate goes by because He just loves you and wants you to have those five dollars. You may laugh at that, but I've had people write in to my ministry saying all sorts of crazy stuff like that!

"Brother Jesse, God told me to leave my husband. He sent me another man who is wonderful, and I know God wants us to be together. I'm married now, but I'm in love with another man and God has given me such a peace about leaving my husband. When I was praying I heard God say, 'I love you and I want you to be happy. Divorce your husband because I've sent another to you.' Oh, Brother Jesse, I feel such a peace about this divorce. My husband isn't too excited about it and he's really mad, but this new man is a blessing from God and my new relationship is just ten times better than the one I had with my husband!" I've actually heard this kind of thing!

God doesn't send people another mate while they're still married! God wouldn't hurt one person in a relationship like that by sending another to them. That's like God being third party to adultery! And He wouldn't do that! God wouldn't tell anyone to leave their husband because they found someone better looking or better talking!

Read His Word and you'll find out that God wants to restore people individually and restore all relationships, not destroy them! Divorce may happen, but it's not His doing or His plan. His plan is always to tug at their hearts so they'll ask Him for forgiveness, then forgive each other, communicate, commit to making the needed changes, and go about living in peace. His plan is to heal the broken hearts, to teach people how to talk and live harmoniously, and to guide people into restored, loving, and better-than-before relationships.

Now, if one person in the relationship doesn't want God's help and wants out of the marriage, then what can the other person do except pray for them and let them go their way? We can't exercise our will over another person's will. People are going to do what they are going to do. But don't drag God into the situation and say He ordained it when it is not in His Word! That's just blaming God for your own relationship problems and for your inability to drop the pride issues. Allow God to come in and work to heal the both of you, and then start working things out through communication and other natural ways of getting along.

It's just crazy to think that God would go against His own Word and His own nature and say something as ridiculous as that! It's His will that you fall back in love with that mate, work out your issues, and have a good marriage.

Know What the Word Says

Sometimes divorce seems like the only option because one person is breaking away or abusing or something. Moses let people divorce, but when people asked Jesus about it, He said that Moses only allowed it because of the hardening of their hearts; originally it was not God's way. In other words, "God didn't mean for you to divorce, but people's hearts are hard towards each other and God, so it happens." When a person has a soft heart towards their mate, they aren't as interested in being right as they are being kind.

God didn't want anyone acting abusive to another person, but people's hearts are hard, and some abuse, misuse, and hurt other people. That is a result of a hardened heart. Hard-heartedness leads to all sorts of destruction in relationships, especially in the marriage relationship. But the hardness of a person's heart can be softened through communication with God.

Healing always begins in the heart.

You must know the Word of God about situations. I can't stand it when people use "God said" as an excuse to do whatever it is they want to do, regardless of what the Word says. I've heard people say all sorts of unbiblical statements and use "God said" as an excuse. God wouldn't tell you to commit murder! God wouldn't tell you to abuse, use, or dishonor anyone around you. He wouldn't tell you to be manipulative. He wouldn't tell you to lie, steal, or cheat.

God is only going to tell you things that are in His nature, and He's a good, just, and honorable God Who keeps His Word. His Word will never lead you wrong! It's alive with His power, and it's one of the many ways God speaks to you.

CHAPTER 10

God Speaks Through Scripture

Have you ever listened to the radio and heard that static as you dial between the stations? A lot of believers are trying to hear God's voice, but there's so much static going on in their minds that they can't hear a thing. That static comes from not being in tune with the Holy Spirit of God within you.

Some people say, "God never talks to me."

I say, "He wrote an entire book to you. Read it!"

How do you get in tune and get rid of the static so you can hear God's voice? One way is to meditate on what God has already spoken in His Word. I believe the most important way God speaks to His people is through the Holy Scripture. His book is His Word to you. As you read, God can reveal Himself to your mind.

How many times have you read a familiar Scripture and all of a sudden, one day, it just leaps off the page? Or you may hear someone quote a Scripture and, although you've heard it many times before, suddenly, it makes sense to you. It makes you think, *Whew! Glory to God!* Something clicks and you have an understanding of what God was saying like you never had before. That is one of the ways God speaks to His people.

That's why He believes that all of us should be reading His Word, even devouring His Word, on a regular basis. It's a way for Him to talk to you! It's a way for Him to talk to me. As we read the Word, God will reveal certain passages to our mind that way. Some people call that getting a revelation, and it simply means that God spoke to your mind by way of a certain passage of Scripture.

There have been so many times I have had this happen to me. I may have read the same verse fourteen thousand times it seems like, and then all of a sudden, one day I read it and *bam!* It's like I just heard it with my ears for the first time!

God's speaking! I'm listening and suddenly I understand. *Whew!* It makes me want to grab a pulpit and kick! I say, "Man! God, that is what You were saying all that time! I get it!"

I love the Word of God. I thank God that I was educated enough to read. Being able to read is a phenomenal blessing I never take for granted. It's a beautiful way God uses to talk to me.

Flying and Reading

God has blessed me with a jet that I use to travel around the nation. It's sort of like my church building, a tool to reach my congregation—except my congregation is spread all over the world! That's the call of the evangelist, and I'm so blessed to have that plane because it helps me do more than I ever did when I had to use the airline's schedules.

Before I had this plane, I flew for fifteen years on the commercial airlines. I flew so much that I had enough Frequent Flyer miles to bring my staff to Hawaii for free. Now, that's a lot of miles! The pastor of the church on Maui found us great condos at a really low cost, and we ended up going to Hawaii for the cost of driving to Biloxi, Mississippi. And we're based out of New Orleans, Louisiana! So that is only an hour and a half up the road! I flew *that* much. I had *that* many miles. I practically lived on a plane.

After so many years, I had a routine that I regularly followed. After I boarded the plane and put my bag in the overhead bin, I'd either grab a magazine or the *USA Today* from the plane's selection of reading materials. Once in a while, I'd get out my Bible and start reading.

Now, when I read the Bible, I don't just try and get in as many chapters as I can. I hear some people brag, "I read five chapters from the Bible every day." I think, *Well, whoop-tee-doo! So what! How many do you remember? How many do you really understand? How much is God talking to you?*

What is the purpose of a person whizzing through reading the Bible? Is it just so they can say, "I've read that book from cover to cover"? Great! But remember that it's what you understand that matters. It's what you apply that is going to make a difference in your-life.

There were many times when I was on a plane that I'd read my Bible and the pages wouldn't turn very often. I'd read a story or a teaching, and then I'd just think about it for a while. I'd read it again and again.

"God Just Created Earth!"

Once I was sitting in the window seat, and there was a man sitting in the middle seat. I picked up my Bible, and I turned to the book of Genesis because that is my favorite Old Testament book. My favorite

New Testament book is the book of Ephesians. I love Ephesians because it encourages me and tells me who I am in Christ. Man, I see myself all over that book!

So on the plane that day, I opened to the first page of the first book and started reading to myself,

> *"In the beginning God created the heaven and the earth.*
>
> *"And the earth was without form, and void; and darkness was upon the face of the deep. And the spirit of God moved upon the face of the waters.*
>
> *"And God said, Let there be light: and there was light.*
>
> *"And God saw the light, that it was good: and God divided the light from the darkness.*
>
> *"And God called the light Day, and the darkness he called Night. And the evening and the morning were the first day.*
>
> *"And God said, Let there be a firmament in the midst of the waters, and let it divide the waters from the waters.*
>
> *"And God made the firmament, and divided the waters which were under the firmament from the waters which were above the firmament: and it was so.*
>
> *"And God called the firmament heaven. And the evening and the morning were the second day.*
>
> *"And God said, Let the waters under the heaven be gathered together unto one place, and let the dry land appear: and it was so.*

"And God called the dry land Earth; and the gathering together of the waters called he Seas: and God saw that it was good."

Genesis 1:1-10

I read that and remembered my study of the original Hebrew text of that passage. The interpreters of the English Bible wrote that God said, "Let there be light," but the original Hebrew is more accurately translated to a simple, "Light be!"

Now, that wasn't the creation of the sun. That came later. Original light was God releasing Himself into nothing. And out of nothing, He would hang something called the earth. So it's God Who is light. First John 1:5 says, *"This is the message which we have heard from him and declare to you that God is light and in him is no darkness at all."* I remembered that in Him there is no darkness, *"...no variableness, neither shadow of turning"* (James 1:17).

I thought, *God releases Himself into nothing, and out of Him, everything I see, touch, smell and eat begins to come into being. But first He has to release Himself because He is the Creator.*

I was sitting in my window seat contemplating that. Now, I can't even count how many times I've read this passage, but I decided to read it again. Suddenly the passage leaped off the page at me, and God began to talk to my mind about His creative power and how the Holy Spirit moved over the deep, doing exactly what God said to do.

The Hebrew text really translates "fluttered." So He was fluttering there over the deep, and when God spoke, He moved and things got done! This was hitting me as so amazing that I turned to the man next to me, looked at him and said, "Wow. Glory."

He just looked up at me.

"What is the matter?"

I couldn't contain myself. I said, "God just created the earth, look!" I pointed to my Bible.

Now, I didn't mean to say that it had just happened, but it came out that way. God was speaking to me through the Scripture, but it didn't come out of my mouth the way it was going into my mind.

Amazed, I said, "It wasn't evolution."

He replied, "Wow, man, you're really into this."

"No," I insisted. "It's into me."

"You seem excited."

"Yes, I am. I am possessed with it!"

He looked at me like I was a freak and said, "Whoa."

"Mister," I said, "I am possessed with a Holy Spirit. It's in me!"

He just froze and looked at me. You see, I had gotten a revelation on a passage I'd read more times than I could count. Suddenly I knew that the same Holy Spirit that lived inside of me because of my salvation was the very same Holy Spirit that fluttered over the deep, acting on behalf of God the Father. The same creative force dwelled in me. It just leaped off the page at me, and I couldn't contain myself.

Fluttering over Mankind

Suddenly, more understanding started to come, and I knew that was how salvation happened too. Before a person gets saved, their life is void. The Holy Spirit is on the outside of them, fluttering over them, waiting for the command to enter and re-create "a new creature in Christ Jesus." It was a revelation of how the Holy Spirit brings light into the life of a new believer.

I understood how salvation would look in the natural and in the spirit realm. In my mind's eye, I saw the Holy Spirit fluttering on top of a man's head, waiting for Jehovah to, in essence, say, *"Light be."* In the natural, the man is reaching out to God, believing in his heart and confessing with his mouth that Jesus is Lord. He's doing it by faith because he sees nothing and he may feel nothing.

But in the spirit realm, the instant he releases his faith, it all starts happening instantaneously: the blood of Jesus comes gushing in, washing away the man's sin; the Father is watching and accepts the sacrifice Jesus made on behalf of the man. He watches as the man becomes a clean vessel. He signals to the Holy Spirit, Who moves from fluttering to inhabiting and *bam!* The Holy Spirit flows from his head to his feet, re-creating the man with His very presence. He is filled with light on the inside, instantly becoming linked to God as family and is a brand new, born-again son of God. Glory!

I believe with my heart that God uses His Scripture to communicate with His children, and that this day, He illuminated the creation Scriptures in order to communicate with me and let me know the magnitude of His regenerative power. And it began with simply reading an old, familiar passage of Scripture.

If you've got a family member that is spiritually lost, I want to share something with you that my mama always said to me when I was unsaved and as lost as a goose in the fog. "Jesse," she'd say, "it's just your tough luck you're related to me, boy! You're getting saved whether you like it or not! I've got the promise of my family down to a thousand generations!" Mama was serious about my salvation, and she was a quick-tempered woman who didn't mince words.

But she had a point. The Bible tells us that God is a faithful Father who keeps His covenant down to a thousand generations of your family! *"Know therefore that the LORD thy God, he is God, the faithful God, which keepeth covenant and mercy with them that*

love him and keep his commandments to a thousand generations"
(Deuteronomy 7:9).

All you have to do is accept that and say, "God, I know you said
that all your promises are yeah and amen, which means yes and so be
it!" Then pray for God to surround them with people who know God.
Pray that God sends them someone they can personally relate to who
will show them the love of Jesus without being threatening.

In your heart, you know that the Holy Spirit is the One Who does
the work. As you pray, the Holy Spirit is fluttering around that lost
one, waiting for them to call on the name of Jesus so He can get His
command from God to move in!

Christian Meditation

Have you ever heard of meditating? Other religions do it all the
time. To get some clarity they might chant something in another
language or use some words that don't mean much but give them
something to concentrate on while they're sitting there on the floor
being quiet and breathing. It's a lot of huffing, puffing, and relaxing to
calm the mind and body.

That's not the kind of meditating I'm talking about.

Christian mediation doesn't concentrate on the physical body as
much and isn't about deep breathing and repeating some mantra to
relax. The focus is on the actual words, and those words are God's
Words. The Bible says that God's Word is a living thing.

It's active.

It's powerful.

And it has the power to change circumstances.

Christian meditation will calm your mind and emotions down. Your body will naturally respond to it, but it's focus is on renewing your mind to what God's Word says. It's about focusing your mind, will, and emotions on the living, active, and powerful Scriptures. And you can do it anywhere or anyway you want.

I meditate on the Word while I'm jogging. Sometimes I just talk to God but a lot of times I'll run over a certain Scripture or series of Scriptures in my mind while I'm exercising. The exercise cleans out my body; the meditation clears my head and feeds my spirit with truth.

Setting aside a portion of time in the day just to pray and meditate on God's Word is a good thing to do. But if you don't have a portion of time to set aside for this, just start wherever you are. If all you have time for is meditating on a few Scriptures during your morning commute, do it. If you can pray and meditate on a Scripture while you're cutting your grass, washing your dishes, doing your laundry, or sitting in traffic, do it then. Thinking about God's Word will help you to clear out the mental and emotional static so you can hear God's voice more clearly.

Chewing, Swallowing, and Digesting

God made us, so He knows what's best for us. That's why He gave us a Bible. The Bible has practical messages to help you out in-life.

Some people think that they're mature Christians because they've been in church for so many years. But maturity comes by how much of the Word you receive and apply in your life—not just by how much-you hear or read. There are a lot of people who've heard Bible teachings for forty years and are still babies when it comes to the things of God. They don't ever let it digest and become a part of their daily living.

Sunday sermons are like food that they put in their mouth, chew a little bit, and then spit out once they hit the door. They never swallow it. Others may swallow it and then throw it up after a few days! Those are some bulimic Christian babies! They never give the Word a chance to digest before they're sticking their fingers down their throat, vomiting up what they heard. Consequently, their lives never really change.

That's why some religious people seem to know so much about the Bible, but they are lost and confused when it comes to really knowing God. The Pharisees you read about in the Bible were like that—a bunch of religious, pious, hard-hearted know-it-alls! Jesus called them "snakes, hypocrites, and vipers" because while they were dogmatically religious, they'd completely lost the spirit of the message. Maybe they never had it! Either way, they weren't digesting much from God! They were just swallowing religious rules and throwing up the heart of God's message.

Getting a Healthy Soul

It just isn't healthy to vomit. It doesn't do your soul a bit of good. The best thing is to hear the Word, chew on it, swallow it, and let it get down on the inside of you so that you can do it! Every Christian really does want to do the right thing. They just get confused within themselves. When their untrained mind takes over, they spit up whatever Word doesn't fit their mind's criteria. This isn't healthy.

First, it's important to know that the "real you" is the combination of your spirit and soul. The Bible says nothing can separate this but the living Word of God. The real you is encased in a flesh body.

Salvation happens when your soul (which is your mind, will, and emotions) decides to accept Jesus as your Redeemer. Then God's Holy Spirit moves in and re-births your spirit so that you can hear God's voice.

The spirit part of you has no problem with the things of God. It's your soulish part (mind, will, and emotions) that you're re-training when you read the Bible. Your mind, will, and emotions are what you use to make decisions in everyday life. Your potential in life is so great, but if your mind is messed up, you aren't going anywhere! Nothing works out when your decisions in life are guided by a messed up mind, will, and an out-of-whack emotional state. The teachings of Jesus help you straighten out your mind, will, and emotions so you can live how God wants you to—in peace, joy, and love.

Jesus' teachings are right there, ready to help you out in life. So eat that Word! Swallow it down, even if it doesn't taste so good sometimes! And as you eat it, swallow it, and digest it, you'll see that it's a better life. Listen, I understand that it's not easy. People think that easy and better mean the same thing. They don't. Sometimes what's easy isn't what's best. Sometimes it's harder to do what's best.

I know some of those Scriptures are hard to hear. Take for instance the Scripture in Matthew 5:44, *"But I say unto you, Love your enemies, bless them that curse you, do good to them that hate you, and pray for them which despitefully use you, and persecute you...."*

Let's just face it. Sometimes you might just want to knock the fire out of somebody! It's hard to bless somebody who is cussing you out. It's hard to do good to those that hate you! And when they are acting like idiots, well, who really wants to pray for them? But you're the better person for it, even if it's tough. It is like a bad tasting vegetable. It stinks and it doesn't taste good, but it's the best one for your body.

Don't ask me why that's the way it is, it just is. Like food is nutritious to your body, the teachings of the Bible are nutritious to the soul. Your mind, will, and emotions become a whole lot healthier when you've been applying what you read in the Bible. Plus, you start hearing God's voice a lot easier too.

CHAPTER 11

When God Speaks Aloud

God talks to His kids in many ways. Probably the most dramatic way God speaks to people is by using an audible voice. Earlier in the book, I told you a testimony of how God spoke audibly to me in my bedroom. Now I'm going to share a biblical story about a young boy named Samuel. This is one of my favorite stories about hearing God's audible voice!

Samuel had a praying mama. Praying women are powerful! The only reason I'm saved today is because my mama and my wife wouldn't give up. They prayed me into the kingdom. Samuel's mother prayed him into existence! The woman was a barren woman. And she didn't like it. Hannah wanted a baby. She prayed and prayed. The woman begged God to bless her with a baby. In fact, she made a promise to God that if He would only give her a son, she'd give the boy back to Him to serve Him all the days of his life.

God honored Hannah's prayer and gave her a beautiful boy who she named Samuel. Hannah kept her word to God, and once Samuel was old enough, she sent him to live and be raised in the house of God with Eli, the priest. His mother loved God so much that she was willing to sacrifice her time with her son so that he would be raised in the admonition of God and in the temple of God. She'd bring him a little coat once each year when she visited the temple.

God honored Hannah with three sons and two daughters after she sent Samuel to be raised in the house of God. Plus, God put a prophetic ministry upon Samuel. That boy grew up to become a great judge of Israel, but he was always known first as a prophet of God.

Something happened to Samuel as a boy that I believe is a good illustration for hearing God's voice. Back in the Old Testament, the people didn't have access to God like we do today because Jesus hadn't yet come. The Holy Spirit dwelled among the people, but He didn't dwell *within* the people, and that made a big difference. They not only didn't have the salvation of Jesus yet, they also didn't have His teachings.

They thought everything good came from God and everything bad came from God. They had no real concept of the devil until Jesus came on the scene. That's one reason why Jesus is called the light of the world. He came to shine a light in a dark place, to expose the devil as "the thief" who'd come to "kill, steal, and destroy." He came to shine a light on God as the good guy and to tell the world that He came *"...that they may have life, and that they might have it more abundantly"* (John 10:10).

Eli's Unruly Kids

Now, Samuel was an Old Testament boy, raised in the church under Eli. Eli was a priest and he had kids of his own. They were bad. They grew up to be young men who slept with the women who were hanging around the temple. They had no respect for the things of God and even ate the communion bread like it was a snack! These boys would munch on the host and drink the communion wine until they got drunk in the church.

Eli wasn't too much of a disciplinarian though, and he let his boys run wild. He'd try and reason with them, but they wouldn't listen to him. Proverbs 22:15 says, *"Foolishness is bound in the heart of a child; but the rod of correction shall drive it far from him."* It doesn't say reasoning drives out foolishness; it says a rod of correction runs it out of the heart of a kid.

Now, I believe in discipline, but if you get enjoyment out of it, you need prayer. There is such a thing as abuse, and it's a sin before God to provoke your kids or abuse them. But there is no sin in discipline. Godly discipline is actually a form of love, and God said you should do it if you're a parent. It takes backbone to stand up and do what's right consistently, in whatever situation you may be in, including raising your kids.

Eli's kids were so unruly and undisciplined that God got involved! He isn't going to let His house be put to shame for too long before He takes some action. Eli, as the high priest, was responsible for his sons.

But he didn't control them, and eventually, things got so bad that in 1 Samuel 2:17,18 it says, *"Wherefore the sin of the young men was very great before the LORD...But Samuel ministered before the LORD, being a child, girded with a linen ephod."*

Sin was ruining the church through the priest's family, and eventually, God had enough. A man of God showed up to lay down the prophecy! Eli's kids were going to bite the dust. The prophet said that a new priest was going to rise up.

According to God, His new priest would *"do according to that which is in mine heart and in my mind and I will build him a sure house; and he shall walk before mine anointed for ever. And it shall come to pass, that every one that is left in thine house shall come and crouch* [bow down] *to him for a piece of silver and a morsel of bread..."* (1-Samuel 2:35,36).

Right after that prophetic word was spoken to Eli, God came down to talk to Samuel. Little Samuel had his first prophecy. When God moves, it goes quick! When He wants something to happen, it's going to happen! First Samuel 3:1 lets us know that the Word of the Lord was rare in those days. Nobody was hearing too much prophecy for the people because sin in the church had blocked out God's voice. Plus, the Word of God wasn't in written form to the fullness of what we have today, so the people didn't read it.

Of course, Jesus hadn't come to wash away sin and people were still sacrificing to atone for sin. So the people relied on the prophets of God to lead and guide them. God begins talking to His next priest, the boy Samuel. First Samuel 3 tells the story, but I'll put my paraphrase on it.

Little Samuel Hears God's Voice

The story begins with Samuel sleeping in his bed. His bed is located in the same room as the priest, Eli. The Ark of the Covenant is-in that room too, and they have this tradition of lighting up seven lamps every night and burning the oil until the early morning. Eli is so old that as the lamps are burning out, he can't see a thing. Samuel is lying down in bed, and right before the lamps burn out, he hears a voice in the darkness calling him.

Believing the voice to be Eli's, little Samuel jumps out of bed and says, *"Here I am!"*

He wants to see what Eli needs. He's an obedient boy and wants to help his priest.

So he ran to Eli and said, "Here I am, for you called me."

Eli says, "Boy, go back to bed! I didn't call you!"

Samuel goes back to bed and he hears the voice again.

"Samuel!"

So, Samuel gets out of bed quickly and again runs over to Eli.

"Here I am, for you did call me."

Eli answers, *"I did not call, my son; lie down again."*

Now, 1 Samuel 3:7 says something odd to me. It says, *"Now Samuel did not yet know the Lord, neither was the word of the Lord yet revealed unto him."* Isn't that amazing that you can be raised in the house of God and yet not know God? That you can be raised in a godly home and still not know God?

> *"And the Lord called Samuel again the third time. And he arose and went to Eli, and said, 'Here am I; for thou didst call me.' Then Eli perceived that the Lord had called the boy"* (v.-8).

Notice that Eli begins to discern something here so he gives the boy instruction on what to do.

> *"Therefore Eli said unto Samuel, Go lie down: and it shall be, if he calls thee, that thou shalt say, Speak, Lord; for thy servant heareth. So Samuel went and lay down in his place"* (v.-9).

In other words, Eli was telling the boy to acknowledge the Lord's voice and to let God know that he can hear Him speaking.

> *"And the Lord came, and stood, and called as at other times, Samuel! Samuel. Then Samzuel answered, Speak, for thy servant heareth"* (v.-10).

Notice Samuel's obedience to Eli's instruction by saying he hears. He is a servant at heart and is submissive to authority. Just as he was so quick to jump out of bed to attend to Eli, Samuel was just as quick to attend to the words of God. This is an important part of little Samuel's character. He's a boy who God can use.

That early morning, Samuel heard his very first prophetic word from God and it was a strong one, confirming the word of judgment on Eli's house that had been spoken just before. Samuel went to bed and he was afraid to tell Eli what God had spoken. Eli sensed this and said, *"Please do not hide it from me. God do so to you, and more also, if you hid anything from me of all the things that He said to you."*

So Samuel told Eli everything that God had said to him, and Eli accepted the word and said, *"It is the Lord. Let Him do what seems good to Him."* Eli was a good man. He just let his kids ruin the house of God. And that couldn't happen, especially when the people didn't have Bibles and they relied on sacrifices to atone for their sin and a holy church to give them instruction.

My point in sharing this story is to show how sin can interrupt the free-flowing conversation between God and man. Continual sin can affect whether or not we hear the voice of God. Samuel's obedient, willing, and jump-to-help character was just what God needed in order to share His word. God needed someone who was willing to say, "Speak, for Your servant hears."

God needs someone who is willing to listen.

CHAPTER 12

You Have an Audience with God

Today we are no longer servants as in the Old Testament. Through Jesus' blood we have been made sons and daughters; we have been adopted into the Holy Family. We are an heir with the Father and a joint heir with Jesus. So, today, if God ever calls on you, all you have to say is, "Lord, Your son is listening" or "Lord, Your daughter is listening."

I encourage myself about who I am in Christ Jesus. I quote Scriptures to myself, and sometimes I just look in the mirror and say, "I am in the family of God. I have been birthed into the kingdom of God because of You, Jesus! Greater is He that is in me than he that is in the world! Even though I serve You, I'm no longer called a servant but I'm called Your son! Thank You, Jesus! What do You want me to do today?"

God put the story about Samuel in the Bible for a reason; and one of His reasons is so that you and I would come along one day, read it, and say, "Yeah, listening really is important to good communication!"

Developing Spiritual Perception

If you want to hear and understand the voice of God more clearly in your life, then you must develop your spiritual perception. Not mental or physical perception, but spiritual perception.

Hearing *and* understanding are the keys to spiritual perception. Some people never hear with their spirit because they're always listening with their mind or their five senses. Hearing God's voice is a spiritual thing, not a mental thing. Others hear God speaking to their spirit, but they don't have any understanding. What good is that?

The Bible tells us in Hosea 4:6 that people are destroyed for lack of knowledge. That is in every area, but the worst is in the spiritual area. A lack of knowledge or understanding of the Word can really mess up people's lives. It's important for us to develop spiritual perception so that when we read what Jesus said, we can let it sink into our spirit and then do it!

Prayer is God's language. So how do we get spiritual perception on the Word? By speaking God's language! Whether that's in your own words or through your Heavenly prayer language of tongues, you've got to be a person of prayer if you want to hear God's voice.

Now, that doesn't mean you have got to spend nine hours on your knees. You can pray standing, sitting down, doing whatever. You don't have to be in a closet. You don't have to do that, but bless God, if you want to you can! Prayer creates spiritual perception so that your ears are quickened to hear the voice of God.

Prayer and reading the Word are the tools to re-train your soul—your mind, will, and emotions. When prayer is a focus in your life, you become "God-minded," so to speak. You're like an antenna catching frequencies. Boy, if God says something, you pick it up immediately! Like young Samuel you jump up and say, "You called?"

As you develop in your prayer life, you get better at receiving because you get a stronger receiver! God could say, "I love you" very softly, and if your receiver is strong, you respond right back, "I love You too, Jesus! What do you want me to do?" He may say, "I just want to talk to you, that's all. I want to show you something in my Word that's going to help you today." You two are communicating. Talking with God is that simple.

Prayer Gives You an Audience with God

When you're born again, you can go boldly to God in prayer. You don't have to tiptoe around. You're His kid. He loves you. He wants to talk with you.

Did you know that Jesus is our High Priest in Heaven? Not only is He that, but He's also our Brother because of the work He did at the cross. And because we're part of the family, we can be strong and bold when we pray. Prayer is the time when you have an audience with God. Hebrews 4:14-16 says this:

> *"Seeing then that we have a great high priest, that is passed into the heavens, Jesus the Son of God, let us hold fast our profession.*
>
> *"For we have not an high priest which cannot be touched with the feeling of our infirmities; but was in all points tempted like as we are, yet without sin.*
>
> *"Let us therefore come boldly unto the throne of grace, that we may obtain mercy, and find grace to help in time of need."*

When you say, "Heavenly Father, I boldly come to the throne of grace in Jesus' mighty name," something happens in the spiritual realm. It's as if the gates of Heaven blow open for you and the red carpet is rolled out, so you can walk right up and talk to God. You can go boldly to the throne when you use the powerful name of Jesus. Every angel bows to that name, and they'll clear the path for you as God says, "Here is one of My sons!" Or, "Here is one of My daughters!"

The reason why some people can't seem to reach God is because they don't have any boldness or confidence, but worst of all, they're just trying to feel Him. They gauge whether He's listening or not by how they feel. Jesus gave you an audience with God when He went to the cross. Your feelings aren't a gauge, telling you whether God is listening or not.

Some people think the goose bumps are God's warning signal that He's in the building. But goose bumps could be there because the air condition just kicked on. It might not have a thing to do with anything spiritual!

Elvis Has Left the Building

When people who gauge God's presence by their feelings lose those goose-bumpy feelings, it's sort of like when Elvis performed and his people would come on the loudspeaker and say, "Elvis has left the building." Those screaming girls would start bawling and feeling hopeless, knowing that they weren't going to see their "king" on stage until the next concert.

Let me tell you something, you don't have to scream your head off trying to get God's attention and gauge whether He's there according to the size of your goose bumps. God hasn't left the building. He never leaves the building. You're the temple of God according to 1 Corinthians 6:19, so if you're saved, God is always in your building! He is accessible, twenty-four hours a day.

Whoo! Whoo! Whoo!

I will never forget this one meeting I was preaching. In the middle of my sermon this woman in the congregation would holler, "Whoo! Whoo! Whoo!" And it was at the weirdest times. Not after I'd just said something others in the church thought was inspiring enough to shout, but in odd places throughout my sermon. I thought to myself, *I've got a crazy one out there,* and I tried to ignore her. But she just wouldn't let up.

"Whoo! Whoo! Whoo!"

So, finally, I had enough and I yelled out, "What are you going 'whoo' for, lady?"

She said, "Look up!"

So I did, and I didn't see anything spiritual. I just saw a bunch of fake birds hung from the ceiling of the church. That wasn't any big deal to me. I travel all over the world and people hang all kinds of decorations up in church sanctuaries. It's common for me to see crosses, banners, plaques, flags, paintings, and statues in church sanctuaries. This church happened to have some birds hanging from the ceiling.

I was expecting something spiritual, like a vision of something supernatural, but I didn't see anything like that so I looked at the woman and said, "What? I don't see anything!"

Then it hit me. I realized what was going on. The church hadn't hung any old type of bird from the ceiling; they'd hung doves to

represent the Holy Ghost. And every time I would say the words
"power" or "Holy Ghost," it seemed to coincide with the air-
conditioning turning on. It would kick on, and the air coming from the
vent would make the doves move. This woman thought it was a sign
from God. "Whoo! Whoo! Whoo!" were her words of choice when
the "presence of God" was in the room.

That's a true story! And it shows how ridiculous it can be to
gauge God's presence by external things. They took the fake doves
down the next week, and the woman left the church. She quit going
because they took the birds down! I'm serious!

Why did they take the birds down? Not because of the woman's
"whooing," but because they realized that the birds were a fire
hazard.-They'd just hung them up not long before my service, and
they didn't realize how hot the lights got after being on for a while.
They worried that the fake doves would catch fire from being under
the heat so long.

Can you imagine what the woman would have done if they caught
fire one Sunday? I would have loved to see that! She would have been
going, "Whoo! Whoo! Whoooaaaahhh! Gawd! Gawd! Gawd! Your
fire is comin' down!"

You see, we don't need to see a fake bird move to know the Holy
Spirit is in the house. God is in us, so He's always in the house, and
all we've got to do is believe God's Word and come boldly to the
throne of grace. Special anointing comes down in my services when
everyone unifies in prayer and faith. Sometimes the physical body
feels the effects of the Spirit of God.

When the anointing of God is in a room, some people will get
goose bumps. Some people will fall under the power of the Spirit.
Some laugh, some cry, some shake, rattle, and roll all over the floor.
But the point is that feelings aren't a gauge for God's presence. God is

with us when we don't feel Him at all. And He's with us when we're shaking, rattling, and rolling too. Never get too caught up in feelings. They aren't trustworthy. God's Word is trustworthy, and He said He'd never leave us or forsake us. (Hebrews 13:5.)

Spiritual perception, not merely physical perception, is a must if we are to hear and understand the voice of the Lord in our life.

CHAPTER 13

Draw Close to God and Be-Fruitful

Prayer is one way you communicate with God about your daily situations and the deep things of His Word. I encourage you to be quick to pray. I don't care how small you think the problem or need is. Pray about it. If it's enough to take up space in your brain, it's worth praying about. If it's enough to have you thinking about it, pray about it. And if it's keeping you up at night, for goodness sake, pray about it!

I pray about almost everything. I might miss a thing or two here and there, but overall I let God know what's going on. Of course, I know He already knows what's going on in my life. But it gets it off my chest to speak it out, and it gives Him a chance to comfort me and to tell me what to do. I pray every day. Sometimes I pray three times a day. Other times I can't count how many times because I talk to God throughout the day.

I'm not religious about my prayer life because I know that the word *prayer* just means talking to God. And I'm a talker by nature. I like to rap, so that's what God and I do. But I've got enough sense to shut up and listen too.

If I Went by My Feelings, I'd Quit!

Sometimes when I'm jogging and I'm on the last leg of a treadmill's course, my body screams at me. It screams, "Jesse! What are you doing, you idiot! Quit! You're old! Who cares! Have a chicken leg and relax!" I pray a little extra then.

I've even had people ask me, "Are you alright?" They see my face flushed red. They see me looking like I'm about to keel over from exhaustion. I say, "I am, but my body's not." They don't understand. They think I'm crazy, but I don't care. I'm not crazy; I'm just not going by my feelings.

You see, I know that I have an intense schedule to keep and that I've already got meetings booked a few years down the road. Sometimes I laugh about that and say to Cathy, "Can you believe that I know where I'm going to be three years from now?!" I know that if I want to keep doing what God's called me to do, I've got to exercise my body.

Now, I flush easily and I sweat hard when I exercise. If I looked at my outward appearance during a hard run, man, I'd quit! But I know what is going on inside of my body. I know my heart muscle is building stronger with every stride. I know my lungs are flooding with oxygen and sweat is cleaning my body of impurities. I know that vigorous exercise is what it takes for me to be healthy. And that exercise must be done on a regular basis for me to succeed at staying anywhere near my normal weight.

Now, if I listened to what my physical body tells me, I'd be lying on the couch watching television instead of preaching. I'd be eating hog crackling, cheese dip, and yellow cake with chocolate icing instead of swallowing vitamins and eating lean meats and vegetables. I'd be five hundred pounds and out of the will of God. I wouldn't be able to keep my extensive preaching schedule carrying a hundred-pound belly around! I've got to keep my body healthy and my soul healthy. Most importantly, I have to keep my spirit in tune with God if I want to fulfill His plan for my life.

Fly-by-Fruiting

One of the things I'm known for all over the world is my joy. To me, it is fun being saved. Some people are saved just enough to be miserable. When I see that, I think it's a shame because knowing God is about freedom, not bondage. Jesus didn't go to the cross so that we would one day believe on His name, accept His grace and forgiveness, and then go on to live miserable lives! No! He came that we might have life and have it in abundance. I don't know about you, but I don't think Jesus was talking about an abundance of depression.

That stuff is from the pit! Joy is a fruit of the Spirit, available to every believer. Jesus told us that it's the devil who steals, kills, and destroys. Jesus calls him a thief. (John 10:10.) What does he steal? Anything he can get his hands on! But I think what he likes to steal the most from believers is the fruit of the Spirit. You've got to watch the boy. Instead of a drive-by-shooting, the devil will try to do a fly-by-fruiting!

The fruit of the Spirit is love, joy, peace, longsuffering, gentleness, goodness, faith, meekness, and temperance. (Galatians 5:22,23.) These are God's attributes, and they're available to you because you're in the family and have His Spirit residing within you. His attributes manifest in our lives when we do what Galatians 5:25 says,

"If we live in the Spirit, let us also walk in the Spirit." That means we ought to be in tune with the Spirit of God within us and cultivate our godly attributes through prayer, reading the Word, and actively using our fruit.

The fruit of the Spirit comes out of our heart. The closer we get to God, the more joyful we become. The closer we get to God, the more loving towards others we become. We have more peace because we know God is our Father and He is taking care of us. We know this because we're in communication with Him.

The closer we get to God on a regular basis, the more longsuffering and gentle we become. It doesn't happen overnight; it comes by consistently allowing His Spirit to dominate our lives. We grow in goodness, faith, meekness, and temperance, or self-control.

Now, some people seem to eat one fruit more than the rest! Others may choose to throw out one fruit entirely! That longsuffering gets thrown out the most! And temperance? Well, that one doesn't always make it too often either! But God meant for us to allow all His fruit to manifest in our lives. He wants us to enjoy all of it!

As we go about our daily lives, it's the fruit that we allow to flow out of our spirit that makes a difference. We choose to allow the love of Jesus that's in our heart to come out. We choose to allow the joy of the Lord that's in our heart to come out. We choose to allow the peace that passes all understanding to come out of our heart. We choose to allow the fruit of patience to manifest, as well as all the rest.

Day by day, we cultivate the fruit of the Spirit in our lives. Each of us is different and will express our fruit in different ways, but we're all entitled to all of it! I may express my joy differently than you do. I may express my love differently than you do. But both of us have the joy and love of God in our hearts. That's part of what we get when we become children of God. When His spirit moves into us and makes us born again, we get His attributes.

Rotten Fruit

Now, the devil knows that love, joy, peace, longsuffering, gentleness, goodness, faith, meekness, and temperance are all the fruit of the Spirit. He hates every one of those attributes because they're part of God's personality.

So how does the devil react to love? By desperately trying to bury a seed of hate in your heart.

The devil responds to spiritual joy with natural depression.

He responds to spiritual peace with natural anxiety.

He responds to spiritual longsuffering with natural impatience.

He responds to spiritual goodness with his natural uncaring and self-centered badness!

Faith is replaced with fear.

Meekness is replaced with arrogance.

Temperance is replaced with unrestraint.

Satan tries his hardest to do a fly-by-fruiting on you by stealing God's precious fruit of the Spirit and replacing it with his own rotten fruit. When you see his attributes in your life, you know that you need to seek God about it.

Pray, read the Word, and make a conscious decision to allow what is already in you to come up out of you! That's why God called it fruit. It's inside you in seed-form, but when you water it with the Word and communicate with God in prayer, that fruit starts growing! Soon you are a tree that is heavy with good, godly fruit!

God's fruit will help you to be victorious in life. The devil will try to pluck off every piece of fruit you're showing, and he'll try and stop the fruit you have inside of you from growing. He doesn't want you showing off your fruit!

Why? Because love, joy, peace, longsuffering, gentleness, goodness, faith, meekness, and temperance are attractive to unbelievers. Every human really wants love. We all want joy and peace. People respond to gentleness. They respond to goodness, faith, and meekness and respect those who have temperance in their lives.

Think about it. Have you ever been drawn to a depressed and miserable person? Some people seem like they like misery, but what they really like is the attention they think it will bring them. That's really a desire for love. Have you seen someone losing control, with no temperance whatsoever, and thought, *Man, I'd like to be just like that guy!* Probably not! The people you meet in life will be drawn to the fruit of the Spirit that is in you; they will most likely be repelled by the rotten, sour fruit of the flesh.

I Like the Fruit of Joy

People always comment on the joy that is in my life. They are drawn to it. But I wasn't a joyful man before I accepted Jesus and began to pray, read the Word of God, and act on its teachings. That's how the fruit of the Spirit grew in my life.

At one time, I had zero patience. Today, I am a thousand times more temperate than I used to be. I used to be easily enraged. I blamed it on my Cajun heritage. I used to say, "I can't help it. I've got Tabasco sauce running through my veins." It was just an excuse to not develop the fruit of temperance in my life. I still mess up from time to time, but God has taken me so far from where I was before.

Before I was saved I wasn't funny. I'll never forget when I preached my first sermon and people started laughing. I got angry because I thought they were laughing at me. Afterwards, I talked to my wife, Cathy, about it and she said, "But, Jesse, you're funny!" I thought, *I don't want to be funny; I want to preach the Word!* I didn't understand that it was a fruit of the Spirit that was manifesting in my preaching. It was just coming out of my heart.

Before I was saved I was a serious, determined, and completely focused man. After I got born again, God used my determination and focus for His benefit. He maintained my seriousness but directed it towards His Word and His call on my life. But He added joy to me that I had never had before. He added peace to me that I'd never had before. He added love for people to me that I never had before.

Before I got born again, I never loved people! I was a rock entertainer, and the only people I loved were the crowds that came to see my band play. I didn't love the individuals. I loved the crowd because that meant I made more money. I'd come from poverty, and success was what I was interested in.

Child-like Faith Works

I realize a lot of people don't believe that I talk to God the way I do and that He talks back, but it doesn't change the fact that He does!

People ask me all the time, "Brother Jesse, does God really talk to you the way He does? Are those stories you tell the truth?" Yes! I talk to God my way, and He talks back to me the way I can understand it. He doesn't speak some other language; He speaks my language! Sometimes He throws a few 'thee's' and 'thou's' in there. I don't know why He does it, He just does. Maybe I hear it better that way sometimes! I don't know!

I'm not preaching in order to convince the skeptics. I'm just telling people what God has done in the Bible and what He will do for them. I can't help it if I am just crazy enough to believe God's Word. Don't blame me! I just believe what He said! That's my child-like faith at work, and it works.

Jesus Never Tried to Convince People

When I read the Gospels, I never read of Jesus urging anybody to believe anything. He said, "When you see Me, you see the Father." End of statement. They said, "We don't believe it." Jesus didn't respond because it didn't make a difference whether they believed it or not. It was still true anyway.

Jesus isn't the Son of God just because people believe He is the Son of God. He is the Son of God whether anybody chooses to believe it or not. End of statement!

I try to follow His example, and I don't try to convince people I hear God's voice. Let the skeptics believe what they want, which will usually be nothing. When they get hit with trouble, they'll be calling out God's name! It always happens that way.

Some people don't want to have anything to do with you if you're a preacher, that is, until tragedy hits. When tragedy hits, people run to God. It's a fact. I've seen it happen on airplanes before. People can be cussing up a storm one minute, but when the airplane starts shaking because of bad weather, you hear them shout, "Oh God!" or "Jesus!"

God's name spoken all over that shaking plane!

Now, I have never heard anyone say, "Oh Buddha! Oh Mohammed! Oh Goddess!"

No, you hear, "Jesus Christ!" or "Oh Jesus!" or "God help us!" Do you ever wonder why? Because in the heart of a person, there really is no unbelief concerning God. People know in their hearts that God exists. They may dismiss it with their intellect, but from their heart they will cry out to God. God knows this, and that's why you never read passages that are trying to really convince you that He exists.

God knows that you already know He exists. People may wander from that, but inside they know. Even an atheist will shout the name of God during a plane crash! It comes out of his heart. It may come in fear. But it comes, believe me!

I personally don't try to convince everyone of what I believe concerning the Word. I just preach what I believe it says. When it comes to more controversial subjects, if someone has a strong opinion that is not mine, I don't nag at them until they concede and say, "OK! OK! I'll believe your way!"

For me, it's not about convincing others. It's about speaking the Word in truth and allowing the person to choose what they'll believe and receive. God gives people a free will in all things, so it's the least we can do to follow His example in this.

If you've got loved ones that you know need Jesus, you've got to realize that all you can do is share what you know with them and pray for them. It's up to them to believe and receive the Word as truth. We must allow people the right to choose what they will believe and never badger them or try to convince them of the truth. But we should never water down what we believe either!

Don't misunderstand me; I don't water down what I believe just because somebody doesn't like it! But I realize that it's their choice and I'm not the one to convict their heart. That's one of the Holy Spirit's jobs, and I'd just mess the situation up if I tried to play God.

All believers should develop spiritual perception through prayer so that God can use us to speak the right words at the right time.

The Power of Understanding

Hearing God's voice and understanding His commands—that's what helps us to have good success in every area of our life. Matthew 13:23 says, *"But he that received seed into the good ground is he that **heareth the word, and understandeth it;** which also beareth fruit, and bringeth forth, some an hundredfold, some sixty, some thirty."*

Sometimes we can hear the wisdom of the Word, but we don't take the time to really pray about it and let it sink down into our spirits so we can have real understanding of it. We're like kids with guns, asking, "Where's the trigger, Mama?" We've got all the power in the world in our hands, but if we don't know how to use it, it is useless to us.

I believe we have the power of God and everything we need to live well in the Bible and the teachings of Jesus. God has given all His power and the authority to use it, but we're still trying to figure out how the trigger works. We're still trying to understand it.

To make people think that they knew something about God, churches came out with all sorts of doctrines. They'd say if you prayed a certain number of prayers, you'd make things right with God. Others said if you'd get baptized in this certain way, then you'll go to Heaven. Still others would say if you believed their particular creed, you'll go to Heaven. If you don't, you're going to Hell.

People say all sorts of things because, while they read the Word and receive the seed, they don't really understand. It doesn't grow well. Therefore there is no fruit or no good result in the end. Don't eat from those kinds of crops. Don't allow yourself to become dogmatic to their doctrine. Their crop doesn't have any nutrition for you. All they've got is bitter stems! No good fruit!

The Scripture in Matthew 13:23 says that we're supposed to *"beareth fruit and bringeth forth...."* This means we should *hear* the Word, seek God to *understand* it, and then "beareth," or act on it, to produce fruit in our lives, and then "bringeth forth," or share, the news with others.

Beareth and Bringeth Forth

Once in my early ministry years, after a church service a lady came up to me and said, "Brother Jesse, I want you pray over me and fill me with the Holy Ghost." I remember that I had just been filled myself. It took me forever to receive that from God!

So I said, "Look honey, I've been waiting on this stuff for years, so you're going to have to get that yourself. I almost killed myself trying to get it! You just go ahead and get it yourself." I'm serious! That's what I said. Why? Because I'd just "beareth" that fruit for myself, but I couldn't "bringeth forth" it for anybody just yet. I had to-get some more understanding first!

In that time of my life, I had people who thought that just because-I was a preacher, I could "bringeth forth" my faith for every fruit out there. No, I could only bring what I had to start with in those early years!

I'll never forget when someone asked me to pray in faith with them for God to give them a million dollars. I said, "Let me tell you something, Jack. If I'm going to believe for a million dollars, I'm going to believe it for myself!" I was honest. I couldn't believe for that with them. I didn't have the faith for it yet, and I was honest enough to say so instead of standing in an empty prayer of "disagreement" with them.

Today I have the faith for that million and more. I've believed it in my own life more times than once, and God has honored my faith in His ability. In fact, my faith has increased and increased the longer I've been walking with God and so has my ability to bring forth what I know to others.

Pass On What You Know

It is so much better to pass on what you know than to keep it to yourself. To be saved is wonderful; but to pray with someone and lead them to the Lord is incredible! To pray in the Holy Ghost is an incalculable gift; but to pray with people to receive the baptism of the Holy Ghost and to watch them speak with other tongues for the first time—well, that'll light a fire under you that can't be put out!

God will send people to you that are hungry for some good fruit. That's what He does for me. I'm known for my joy. God sends the most depressed people to me, and then they pick an apple of Holy Ghost energy off of me and eat a little. That taste of God's joy puts a little zing of joy into their walk with Jesus.

They'll say, "Man, Brother Jesse! You just make me laugh and stir me up!" I say, "That's because you're eating some of my fruit." Joy is a fruit of the Spirit, and I've got lots of it!

Are You Listening?

You can do a lot of things that people tell you to do. Great men and women of God have been given revelation knowledge on many subjects in the Bible. But if you hear them and it does not drop into your spirit, it will never give you the desired results. The Word has to be heard, not just with the ears, but also with the spirit.

I have learned something as I've been growing in the Lord and it's this: Listening to God is the most important thing you can do. Now, sometimes God tells me stuff I don't want to hear. Little Samuel didn't want to hear what God told him. He loved Eli and didn't want to speak that word of confirmation.

I don't like everything God tells me, but it doesn't change what He said. I've got to listen to God. You've got to listen to God—and that means everything He tells you to do. If you don't, eventually you are going to get caught up in that disobedience, and then disobedience will make you fall in life.

Whether it is spiritual, physical, or financial, when you disobey God, you leave yourself wide open. Not wide open to the devil's attacks, because he attacks anyway, but open to fall or to give in to his temptation and be led astray.

CHAPTER 14

Jesus Hears God's Audible Voice

Sometimes when a person hears God's audible voice, it catches the devil's attention. The devil is no fool, and he knows that a person who has heard God's voice is going to be fired up and want to share God's message with others.

The devil doesn't want that happening. So he's quick to try and steal whatever good thing was deposited in the heart of the hearer. He-may attack or tempt unmercifully in the hopes that the believer will doubt God, fall into disobedience, and become ineffective in telling their message. This temptation even happened to Jesus after His baptism.

You see, Jesus wanted to be baptized, but He had a hard time getting John to do it. John was Jesus' cousin and he didn't think he was worthy enough to baptize Jesus.

Matthew 3:13,14 says, *"Then cometh Jesus from Galilee to Jordan unto John, to be baptized of him. But John forbad him, saying, I have need to be baptized of thee, and comest thou to me?"*

But Jesus wouldn't take no for an answer. It was His baptizing day, and that was going to be that! *"And Jesus answering said unto him, 'Suffer it to be so now: for thus it becometh us to fulfil all righteousness.' Then he suffered him"* (v. 15).

In other words, "I know it doesn't seem right, but do it anyway because we've got to fulfill My Father's righteous plan." So John did it. Meanwhile, God is up in Heaven watching all this. This is how the Bible tells it:

"And Jesus, when he was baptized, went up straightway out of the water: and, lo, the heavens were opened unto him, and he saw the Spirit of God descending like a dove, and lighting upon him:

" And lo a voice from heaven, saying, This is my beloved Son, in whom I am well pleased."

Matthew 3:16,17

I mean, here God is sitting in Heaven watching His Son being baptized and *wham!* Jesus comes straight up out of the water, the Holy Spirit falls on Him like a dove, and God starts yelling all the way from Heaven! He says, and I'm paraphrasing, "Hey everybody! That's My Boy and I love Him! I'm proud of Him!" That's a proud Papa God.

The Father just can't contain Himself at Jesus' baptism. He wants the world to hear it with their actual ears that this man is His Son and He is pleased with Him.

Now, something happens when you fulfill God's plan like Jesus did. Something happens when the Holy Spirit of God falls on you and God hollers from the throne that He's proud of you!

You get attention.

In Jesus' case, He got attention from the people watching the baptism. They all heard God's voice that day. But He also got attention from the devil.

Attention from the Devil

The last Scripture in Matthew 3 is verse 17. It records God's audible words over Jesus at His baptism. Do you know what the very first verse of Matthew 4 says?

"Then was Jesus led up of the Spirit into the wilderness to be tempted of the devil" (v.1).

So Jesus gets out of the water, and the next thing you know He's walking into the wilderness at the leading of the Holy Spirit. Now, the devil doesn't come to tempt Jesus right away. He waits a while. Now, I've been to the Holy Land and I've seen the wilderness this Scripture mentions, and it's not a lush forest. It's sand dunes and rocks, and there's nothing refreshing about it. Jesus was out there alone in the wilderness for forty days and forty nights.

"And when he had fasted forty days and forty nights, he was afterward an hungered" (v. 2).

What is Jesus doing for those forty days and nights? He's fasting. He's preparing. And just when He gets super-hungry, the devil comes with his temptations. First, He tempts Him to turn the stones into bread. Satan is slick. Notice, He doesn't come to chat when Jesus was strong, right after He's just been baptized, had the Spirit descend on Him, and heard His Father's audible voice. He waits until Jesus is in a weakened physical state of hunger. He starts with food.

Then He moves on to tempt Jesus about His Father's saving love. He brings Jesus to the highest pinnacle of the temple and tempts Him to jump off in order to test God and see if He loves Jesus enough to save Him.

Lastly, the devil tempts Jesus with everything he has. He offers to give all his great kingdoms of the world, with all their glory, if only Jesus would do one little thing—fall down and worship the devil in private. This would have made Jesus a king over the kingdoms and would have afforded him every luxury known to a king.

Jesus doesn't bite the bait. He resists the temptation and rebukes Satan over and over again. In Matthew 4, Jesus responds to the first temptation saying, *"But he answered and said, It is written, Man shall not live by bread alone, but by every word that proceedeth out of the mouth of God"* (v. 4).

To the second temptation He replies, *"It is written again, Thou shalt not tempt the Lord thy God"* (v. 7).

Then to the third temptation He rebukes, *"Get thee hence, Satan: for it is written, Thou shalt worship the Lord thy God, and him only shalt thou serve"* (v. 10).

Three strikes and you're out, devil!

Notice that Jesus always quoted the Word to the devil in response to the temptations. Why? Because even Jesus knew that to win at battling temptation, you've got to speak the Word. That's what works.

When he tempted Jesus with food, Jesus probably thought, *I made it for forty days without bread, devil. What? You think I can't make it another day? Get lost!*

And to try and trick Him into committing suicide? Jesus must have thought, *Devil, you're living in a dream world! I'm not stupid enough to jump off the church! I'm not tempting God!*

And the last temptation? That's one the devil would have loved to see work. To be worshiped was what the devil wanted, and he was willing to give up everything for that. But Jesus wasn't about to do that. He knew Who His Daddy was! He may not have been honored and presiding over all the devil's kingdoms yet, but His Father made the world and had a plan to set things right again.

Jesus would soon be the King of kings and the Lord of lords. .The Cross was coming, and soon, the redemption plan would be in effect. And He also knew that later on in time, He would be coming back again, to continue God's plan for this earth and to fulfill all the end-time prophecies. Jesus knew God's plan for man and He knew His own future, so He wasn't about to accept the devil's offer for a counterfeit reign.

Matthew 4:11 says that after the temptations, *"Then the devil leaveth him, and, behold, angels came and ministered unto him."* The-angels had to come and minister to Jesus because He'd just been through an ordeal.

And it all started right after He heard God's audible voice saying,-*"...This is my beloved Son, in whom I am well pleased"* (Matthew 3:17).

There is a lesson in that. First, it shows us how concerned the devil was about seeing the Son of God on the earth. He was worried. He'd been having virtually a free reign on the earth and was pretty shaken up by the idea of God sending His Son to the earth.

Put that idea right beside your mind's eye picture of God hollering from the throne over His extraordinary love and pride for Jesus, and you can really see good and evil side by side.

It shows you the encouraging, loving manner of God and the deceiving devil who takes notice when He speaks.

CHAPTER 15

The Inner Witness

Another way God speaks to His people is to their spirit through what's called an "inner witness." Years ago, I woke one morning with a severe heaviness on my heart. I felt fine physically. My ministry was doing wonderful, and everything was great in my personal life. No problems anywhere, and no one in particular was on my mind.

Everything was just fine. And yet, I had this heaviness on my heart, a sense in my spirit that not all was well. I don't know how else to explain it except to say it was like one, big "blah" on my heart. Have you ever had that happen to you? Have you ever woken up and you are not sick or anything of that nature in terms of physical symptoms that you can see in your body, but you've just got that sense of heaviness on you? Well, I did that morning.

I tried to shake it off, but it just wouldn't go. It wasn't physical, emotional, or mental heaviness. I knew it was spiritual. So I figured that since it was heavy, it was from the devil, and I began to rebuke him for trying to oppress me.

I said, "Devil, I come against you in the name of Jesus. I bind you, because the Bible says that if I bind the strongman, then I can enter into his house and take his possessions. I bind you, devil from Hell. Get out of here!" But nothing changed and the sense of heaviness only got worse and worse.

There wasn't a thing wrong with me, so I kept on binding the devil for about thirty-five minutes. Man, I had more knots bound up in that rope than you can shake a stick at!

Finally, I stopped binding and started praying, and then I heard a quiet, audibly silent but definitely there voice going into my heart. I knew that voice; God was speaking to me.

"Jesse."

"What?"

"What are you doing? Why are you are binding Me?"

"I am binding You, God?"

"Yes," He said, "I am using your spirit right now, with utterings and groanings that cannot be mentioned. I'm using your spirit to make intercession."

Ah, I got it. God was teaching me something. I'd read the Scripture in Romans 8:26 that says, *"...for we know not what we should pray for as we ought: but the Spirit itself maketh intercession for us with groanings which cannot be uttered."*

Now, the Holy Spirit inside of me was using my spirit to pray intercessory prayers just like the Scripture said. It wasn't about me. It wasn't for me. The Holy Spirit had decided to team up with my spirit to pray because obviously, somewhere our combined prayers were needed.

Wow, I thought, *I'm making groaning intercession.*

It must have been one heavy-duty intercession session because my heart felt like it'd been run over with a truck. I don't know who God was praying for through me. It might have been somebody in China. It could have been someone who lived down the block. It could have been you. It could have been for me. But all of a sudden, I felt it lift. I went, *"Whew."* I realized that God was using me. He was speaking through me for someone else.

It's a form of communication He uses, to speak directly to the spirit of an individual to let them know that there is something going on that deserves deep prayer. He does it that way because *"...we know not what we should pray for as we ought"* (Romans 8:26). We don't know how to pray about it like we should with our minds, so the Holy Spirit surpasses our mind and goes right to our spirit, where He starts to *"...maketh intercession for us with groanings which cannot be uttered"* (Romans 8:26).

I've asked congregations in my travels to raise their hands if this experience has ever happened to them. Not as many people respond to this question as those who say God communicates with them through Scripture. Perhaps that's because many feel that heaviness and end up rebuking the devil, like I did. Or, perhaps, they just don't think that the heaviness in their spirit is the Holy Spirit's call for the prayer of intercession.

Prompted to Stop and Pray

Another way this works is when the Holy Spirit within you is trying to alert you to something. For example, do you ever go to church and nobody seems to be able to really praise and worship like they usually do? It may be normally very easy to enter into worship to God, but somehow today no one can worship very well? Maybe it just seems like a dead worship service?

I've had this happen during my meetings before. If I'm the host and the worship team playing the music is my band, then I just tell them to stop. I may let them finish the last song, but then I get up and tell them to play a certain song, one that is simple and easy for the people to sing along with. Then I tell the congregation to pray.

When a united body of believers begins to pray, whatever is in the way will either (1) break under the power of prayer, or (2) be revealed by the power of the Holy Spirit. Either way, the Holy Spirit is giving everyone the inner clue that something needs to be done. He is prompting everyone to stop and pray.

Alerted by God

Other times, you may wake up in the middle of the night and have a deep sense of urgency to pray. This is a way God communicates with you to let you know that someone needs your prayers right now. It's a task that is divinely given to you to perform.

You may not know the person you're praying for. You might sense no specific person or circumstance, but you have an urgency to pray right then and there. Or, the Holy Spirit may give you divine insight into the situation or person you are praying for. You might even feel like you ought to get up and do something about it.

That hard-to-describe sense of urgency in a person's spirit to pray or do something is one way God communicates with people. It's an alert system He put in place, and it can get stronger the more you obey it. Sometimes His alarm is loud. Other times it's very soft but persistently going off so that you can't ignore it.

If God ever speaks to you in this way, it's important not to ignore it. The person or circumstance is obviously important enough for Him to sound an alarm. It could be a life-and-death situation, and your obedience to pray or act could make the difference.

CHAPTER 16

Supernatural Words of Wisdom-and Knowledge

In charismatic churches, you often hear people saying, "Brother So-n-So gave me a word last night at church." For those of you who don't know, this is called receiving a "word of knowledge" or a "word of wisdom."

What are those "words" from God? They're gifts of the Holy Spirit that God uses to communicate with us. These divine gifts are mentioned in 1 Corinthians 12:8-10 and 12:28. It is when God uses someone else to give you His divine message.

The word that God speaks to you through another person may be a supernatural revelation of His will or plan. It may be a supernatural insight or understanding of circumstances in your own life. It may simply be a word of encouragement for you during a difficult time, or it could be a word given to guide you to act wisely. It could be a divine perspective on what's going on in your life. This way of communication deals directly with your soul (your mind, will, and emotions).

Now, some people think that God doesn't like our soul. They think God would prefer if we were like robots, but that is just not true. God loves the soul! He created it. And besides, it's where the decision is made to accept salvation. God loves your mind, will, and emotions and just wants to see this vital part of who you are strong and healthy. That's another reason He wants unbelievers to know Him.

Without God's presence and His principles for living, our mind is heavy and burdened, our will is either weak or pointed in the wrong direction, and our emotions are unbalanced and unstable. God knows that we can be this way, and He wants to help us have a good life. And you just can't have that without a healthy soul. So He talks to you this way sometimes to help you out in life.

If you've ever had someone come up to you in church or someone at the pulpit call you out of your seat to give you a "word," you know that it can be a pretty exciting time. It can also make you feel a little nervous. You're usually either thinking, *Wow! What does God have for me?* Or, you shift into judgment mode and think, *Now, is this a flaky Christian talking to me, or a real word from God?*

Of course, we should respect the way God speaks through words of knowledge, wisdom, and prophecy. But we should also realize that the Bible is the final authority for governing our lives. Even though a word may come from God and it may give you great encouragement or direction, we must understand that it's still being relayed through a human being. And none of us is perfect. Knowing this, it's natural for your mind to want to check it out.

If you don't know the Word of God, you can listen to a deceiving word and live a lie and not even realize it. You remember that the Bible says in Hosea 4:6 that people are destroyed because of their lack of knowledge. What lack of knowledge destroys us the most when it comes to spiritual matters? Knowledge of the Word of God!

If you stay close to God by reading His Word and talking to Him often, you will have a much easier time knowing what's from Him and what's not. If you have an intimate relationship going on with God, you'll immediately know in your spirit if the word being spoken to you is a message from God or just the good intentions of a misguided believer.

The bottom line is that there are some believers out there who sincerely think they're hearing God but they aren't. Consequently, many Christians have come to be leery about automatically accepting whatever a person says God told them.

It's good to be cautious. You need to be wise! A wise person accepts what is good and known to be from God, and throws out what is bad and known to be human error. Now, if a word is bringing nothing but confusion and doubt, throw it out. I call that separating the wheat from the chaff, and it's a good thing to do. The Bible confirms that confusion doesn't come from God when it says, *"For God is not the author of confusion, but of peace, as in all churches of the saints"* (1 Corinthians 14:33).

Word from a Young Preacher

Many years ago, a young preacher approached me with a word of knowledge. He was just starting out and seemed to look up to me. He just kept blubbering all over himself trying to tell me how much he liked my ministry.

"Oh, Brother Jesse," he said, "I just love your ministry, Brother Jesse. I tell you one thing, you've helped me so much. You are such a blessing to me."

I said, "Well, thank you." He interrupted, "I want to be just like you, Brother Jesse, just like you!"

"Stop," I said. "You don't want to be like me, because I make mistakes. You want to be like Christ, because He doesn't make any mistakes. But I thank you for letting me know how much you like my ministry."

He nodded, nervously looked at me, and spoke again, "Brother Jesse, I don't know if this is the voice of God or not, but God's got a word for you. I believe God gave me a word for you."

I thought to myself, *Well, boy, if this is good, I am going to accept it, put this on the shelf in my mind, and pray it works out. If I'm unsure about it, I'll just keep it on the back shelf in my mind. And if it just doesn't bare witness with my spirit at all, I'll throw it out and go about my business.* Hey, don't get mad at me for thinking that way. Lots of people do!

So I looked at the kid and said, "OK, give me what you got."

He said, "I don't know, Brother Jesse. You judge it."

I thought to myself, *I most certainly will.* But I said, "What has the Lord told you?"

Nervously, he began, "I don't know if it is God or not. I am just young in this stuff but I just want you to listen to it. The Lord told me to tell you that the devil just can't stand before you. You run over him. You kick his head off. You just run at him with everything you've got and you beat him."

I thought, *Now, this kid has got it together! Come on, boy! Give me some more!*

He said, "You just run over him. Every time he sticks his ugly head up, you just bind him and walk on to do the things God told you to do."

Great! I thought, *You're right on, boy!*

Then he went on, "Does that bare witness with you, Brother Jesse?"

"Son," I said, "that's revelation knowledge. You are right."

"OK, now I'll tell you what else God told me. God told me that the devil has stopped getting in front of you and he started getting behind you. He has started to push you harder saying, 'Come on, boy, preach, Jesse, preach. Sleep, why should you sleep? You are a faith man; you don't need to sleep. There are people dying and going to Hell, and you are trying to rest your body. What is wrong with you? Get up, go preach this Gospel. There are people dying and going to Hell right now, and you need to get out there. You don't need to sleep. You don't need to rest.'"

He paused and I don't know if my jaw was hanging out or not, but I just stood there listening.

He continued, "You see, Brother Jesse? The devil can't defeat you in front of you, so he has gotten behind you and started pushing you. Is that right?"

The kid was on the button. I just nodded because I knew that it was from God. You see, at the time, I was averaging about two and a half hours of sleep per night. I was preaching non-stop, every night and up to five times on Sunday with the multiple services. When I'd get to my hotel room, I wouldn't allow myself to rest. I'd read my Bible, watch television, and prepare sermons or whatever. I was always moving.

When I did go to bed, I'd lie there and allow my mind to race through everything I needed to do, wanted to do, or had already done. I felt the pressure to preach, preach, and preach some more. I felt the pushing to go and go. I didn't think that was from the devil. I thought it was just my tenacity to do what God told me to do.

When I was home, my wife just had to pour me in to the bed. I was beat to pieces. The next morning, I would wake up after two hours sleep and give my all again. My body was wearing out but I wasn't listening to it. I wasn't stopping. I was living an unwise life for a man of God.

I'll never forget the last thing that young preacher said. He ended his word from God for me by saying, "Brother Jesse, you won't complete your ministry until you learn how to rest your body."

Whoa! When God speaks as clear as that, you don't have to weigh it for an hour to be sure it's from Him. I simply said, "Thank you. It was from God and I receive it." He shook my hand and left.

Now, that was a young preacher who was just starting out. I'd been preaching for years. God used that young boy to pass an important word of wisdom to me. And as I began to think about that word of wisdom, I recalled the times God had sent others to tell me to rest. I remembered how certain ministers who I esteemed highly in the faith had told me I needed to rest. I respected them greatly when it came to spiritual matters, but I couldn't receive this practical wisdom.

I remembered that one of them had said, "The Lord told me to tell-you to sleep, Jesse." I don't know why I didn't listen to that. I just couldn't be reasoned with because rest just wasn't important to me. I had a job to fulfill for God. I felt pressure to keep up my pace and never quit.

Even my wife would ask me, "Jesse, why won't you rest?"

"Rest, woman? Rest is for the weary! I ain't weary!"

"But Jesse," she'd say, "you look ten years older than you should. You need to rest."

"I'd rather burn out than rust out!" I'd say.

As I considered all this, I suddenly began to think about my body and how it had been giving me troubles. I'd been having chest pains and I was ignoring them. God had even talked to me about it when I prayed, but I wouldn't listen.

So when He couldn't get to me through my spirit and He couldn't reach me through those I respected in the ministry, or even my wife, He sent a young preacher to talk to me, to share the scenario with me, to appeal directly to my soul (mind, will, and emotions), and to make a change. And when my mind saw the spiritual scenario this young man painted for me, I understood and accepted God's warning.

Now, I'm not as bad as I used to be, but it's still a struggle sometimes to make myself slow down. I find myself speeding up again, and then I remember the word of wisdom, and I rest my body. But let me tell you something, it takes a lot more rest to get rested today than it did all those years ago when I heard this word because I'm older now. But I try to get enough sleep each night, and since then, God has provided me with a plane that helps me keep my busy schedule while being home almost every night to sleep in my own bed. That makes a difference.

I hardly ever preach five services on Sunday anymore unless God makes it clear to me that it's what *He* wants me to do. But it's rare. I've learned to accept that He is my Creator, He knows my body, and His plan is the best plan for my life.

CHAPTER 17

God Speaks Through Prophecy

Another gift of the Holy Spirit that God uses to speak to His people is the gift of prophecy. (1 Corinthians 12:8-10, 28.) This is also sometimes just simply called "getting a word." The difference is that when you get one of these, it's future-based and God is using someone to proclaim what He has planned.

Words of prophecy are often strongly delivered and are sometimes delivered by a prophet of God. The five-fold ministry of God, which is sort of like God's executive branch of government, is listed in Ephesians 4:11,12: *"And he gave some, apostles; and some, prophets; and some, evangelists; and some, pastors and teachers; For the perfecting of the saints, for the work of the ministry, for the edifying of the body of Christ."*

But just like an evangelist isn't the only one who can lead someone in the prayer of salvation, so a word of prophecy doesn't have to only come from a prophet. Anyone who is filled with the Holy Spirit, according to 1 Corinthians 14:31, can give prophetic words that teach and comfort as God speaks to them: *"For ye may all prophesy one by one, that all may learn, and all may be comforted."*

God may use this way of talking to you to speak something good about your future and encourage you to keep close to Him to see it fulfilled. This isn't a psychic at work! It's God at work!

Some people hear a word of prophecy and think that it will happen regardless of what they do. This isn't true. It's not about fate. It's simply God telling you, "This is my plan for you. Stick with me, don't get off track, and you will see it come to pass."

If you move away from God and decide not to obey Him, you're putting your will over His will. You will not be going in the direction of God's plan for your life anymore, and so the prophecy will most likely not come to pass.

But if you just stay on track with God, you'll see that prophecy come to pass. It doesn't mean you go and live in a monastery somewhere; it just means you live your life normally but include God in it every day. Read your Bible, try to do what it says, pray, and treat others like you want to be treated.

False Prophets

In the Old Testament Scriptures of Deuteronomy 13:1-5, you'll see that there were many false prophets who delivered signs and wonders in order to draw believers away from God and the teachings of the Bible. The bottom line is that whatever guides you to something other than the truth of the Bible is not from the Holy Spirit. True prophecy will always be in agreement with the Bible.

In the New Testament, it says that there are three distinct purposes-for prophecy today. They are (1) edification, (2) exhortation, and (3) comfort. *"But he that prophesieth speaketh unto men to edification, and exhortation, and comfort"* (1 Corinthians 14:3).

Edification means to build or confirm, and exhortation means to give consolation or solace.

To judge whether a prophecy is from God, you could ask yourself these types of questions: Does the prophecy build me up? Does it confirm something I have already heard from the Lord? Does it give me consolation? Does it comfort me? False prophecy condemns, comes out of "nowhere," and gives you the opposite of comfort. True prophecy will always edify, exhort, and comfort you.

Another thing true prophecy does is bring liberty or freedom into the life of the person receiving it. Second Corinthians 3:17 confirms this when it says, *"Now the Lord is that Spirit: and where the Spirit of the Lord is, there is liberty."*

False prophecies bring the opposite of liberty or freedom into our lives. They bring bondage! But we know by Romans 8:15 that God doesn't promote bondage: *"For ye have not received the spirit of bondage again to fear; but ye have received the Spirit of adoption, whereby we cry, Abba, Father."*

First Corinthians 14:33 also says, *"For God is not the author of confusion, but of peace, as in all churches of the saints."* So you can also ask yourself: Does the prophecy bind me up and give me fear? Or does it loose me of my fears and give me freedom and liberty? Has it brought confusion into my life, or peace and surety?

Another good way to check on the validity of a personal prophecy is to check out the one who is giving it. Jesus warned us about false prophets in this passage of Scripture:

"Beware of false prophets, which come to you in sheep's clothing, but inwardly they are ravening wolves.

"Ye shall know them by their fruits. Do men gather grapes of thorns, or figs of thistles?

"Even so every good tree bringeth forth good fruit; but a corrupt tree bringeth forth evil fruit.

"A good tree cannot bring forth evil fruit, neither can a corrupt tree bring forth good fruit.

"Every tree that bringeth not forth good fruit is hewn down, and cast into the fire.

"Wherefore by their fruits ye shall know them."

Matthew 7:15-20

Another tip can be found in 2 Peter 2:1-3. There it says that false teachers can be recognized when they speak *heresies* and exploit others by making *merchandise* of them.

When it comes to judging prophecy, it's good to know that you've always got the Holy Spirit to help you discern what's true and what's false. First John 2:20 should give you some serious comfort. It says, *"But ye have an unction from the Holy One, and ye know all things."* The word *unction* means the same thing as the word *anointing*, and concerning prophecy, it relates because it shows us that as believers, we have the anointing to discern *all* things.

If you receive a personal prophecy and have a quickening in your spirit that says something is just not right, it is important that you do not discount your "unction." Instead, function in the unction! Allow the Holy Spirit in you to flow and help you to discern whether the prophecy is from the Lord or not.

Remember, although there are false prophets out there, sometimes it is unwitting Christians who allow themselves to listen to other spirits and repeat words that are not from God. It doesn't mean they are all devils from Hell! It just means they listened to the wrong spirit and missed it. Other times false prophecies come by way of Christians who get so excited that they're hearing from God that they decide to chime in and add a little of their own opinion!

You know this is happening when you're given a word that is in line with what God is doing and "right on target" in the beginning, but-then takes a detour along the way and ends up wrong as a three-dollar bill! When this happens, don't let it worry you. Just receive what is good and throw out what is bad, knowing that the one prophesying is human and got carried away. As a blood-bought child of God, you are anointed and fully able to recognize what is of God and what isn't of God.

Counterfeit Words Aren't God's Plan

Sometimes there are people who don't know God but still may be able to tell you about events in the future. But be assured, they aren't getting the information from *your* God.

They've had these people in Bible times too, and the Word tells us that they have "familiar spirits." The familiar spirits that are within them or around them tell them what lies ahead. Leviticus 19:31 warns us, *"Regard not them that have familiar spirits, neither seek after wizards, to be defiled by them: I am the Lord your God."* Wizards of the Bible times were those who conjured up ghosts.

God said:

"There shall not be found among you any one that maketh his son or his daughter to pass through the fire, or that useth divination, or an observer of times, or an enchanter, or a witch,

"Or a charmer, or a consulter with familiar spirits, or a wizard, or a necromancer.

"For all that do these things are an abomination unto the Lord: and because of these abominations the Lord thy God doth drive them out from before thee.

"Thou shalt be perfect with the Lord thy God."

Deuteronomy 18:10-13

There were all sorts of practices in Bible times that God didn't want His people doing or taking part in. The names for the practices may have changed today, but the instruction from God has stayed the same. Most people know in their hearts these things are wrong before God. But just to simplify it all, God spelled out what you're supposed to avoid.

Making your kids go through fire is an obvious wrong. Using divination meant consulting oracles or mediums who were like the prophets of other gods. They were supposed to talk to the gods, and then tell you what they said. Charmers were those who sought to fascinate by means of casting spells. Those with familiar spirits told the future. Necromancers made their life out of seeking out dead people's souls. All this stuff is just the devil's way of counterfeiting God's perfectly good ways of speaking to His people. Following after the devil's counterfeit practices is not God's will for your life.

The last part of the Scripture passage lets you know that you don't-need any of that stuff to be perfect in God's eyes. The word "perfect" is translated from the word *tamiym* which means to be "entire (literally, figuratively or morally); also (as noun) integrity, truth: KJV-- without blemish, complete, full, perfect, sincerely (-ity), sound, without spot, undefiled, upright (-ly), whole."

To be entire means you're complete. To have integrity and know truth, to be an upright person who is sincere and sound—that is what God wants you to be!

CHAPTER 18

Give All the Glory to God

God focuses on the supernatural. Man tends to focus on what is spectacular.

It is the spectacular that brings glory to man but it is what is supernatural which brings glory to God. When God speaks through a person, it's God Who should get the glory for the word—not the man or woman relaying it.

Although the supernatural gifts of the Holy Spirit are wonderful and we should be excited about it when they happen, we shouldn't focus on the person relaying the message. We should focus on God. If the focus is only on the one who is relaying the message, then people will look to that person instead of God. And that's not good.

Sometimes I see ministers on television whose program only consists of showing those who've received words from the minister or healing through a man's ministry. There is no sermon preached, there is no Bible reading or teaching, and there is no worship of God. There is only miracle after miracle or word of knowledge after word of knowledge. It's wonderful to see people healed and it's great to see people flowing in the gifts, but to only focus on the miracles without the Word tends to bring glory to the man.

Jesus didn't do that, instead He always gave the glory to His Father. He is a great healer, and yet He chose to stick with the supernatural instead of merely the spectacular. If you read through the Gospels, you'll see Him saying "Tell no man" over and over again. In other words, "Shut up about it!" Why would He say this? In order to avoid drawing attention to Himself.

I think one reason He didn't want attention was because He knew He was headed to the cross, and He didn't want to go earlier than He needed to! Those Pharisees were flat mean and they didn't like Jesus getting the attention of the people because they wanted to keep the power in their hands. They didn't want Jesus having the power of public behind Him. Jesus had a job to do when He was on the earth, and didn't want the power-hungry Pharisees getting in the way of fulfilling His call.

But you'll also notice as you read through the Gospels how often Jesus made reference to His Father. He did it all the time. They'd say, "Oh, Jesus, You're a great miracle worker." And He'd say, "It's not Me that does the work; it's My Father that does the work." He dealt with the supernatural, but He didn't deal with the spectacular.

Jesus didn't put on a theatrical event, flash lights, and call everyone up who'd ever been healed through His ministry. When I see this done by ministries today, I ask myself, "What is the motive? Why is the miracle being shown or spoken about? Is it to show people that by Jesus' stripes they are healed and bring glory to God? Or is it to show that this particular person has a spectacular ministry?"

Jesus healed but He preached too, and above everything, He continually gave glory to the Father. He continually shifted the attention to the Father. He taught us to do this with His words and through His example.

That means we should give the glory to God at every opportunity we have. If a healing happens, give glory to God. If a word comes forth, give glory to God. If you have a word to give, give it and give glory to God.

Giving a Word

When you're speaking for God, as with giving a word of knowledge, wisdom, or prophecy, be careful of what you are saying. You are handling holy words. So you shouldn't add to what God is giving you or leave something out.

And if you receive a word of knowledge, wisdom, or prophecy, you shouldn't change your whole life based on that word either! Man, don't ever make that mistake! Building your life on the gifts of the Spirit, either through giving words or receiving them, is really unwise because you're dealing with people, and sometimes people miss it or add something to what God said. You don't throw it all out because it's from God and can help you in life. But don't make giving or receiving words your primary way of talking to God either.

The Bible is called the "Word of God" for a reason. It's a book of-God's words to people. Second Timothy 3:16,17 says, *"All Scripture is given by inspiration of God, and is profitable for doctrine, for reproof, for correction, for instruction in righteousness: That the man of God may be perfect, thoroughly furnished unto all good works."*

Think of it like this: your main meal is the Scripture, and words of knowledge, wisdom, and prophecy are like supplements or side dishes to that meal. They're additional ways God nourishes, guides, encourages, and inspires us in life.

I love the gifts of the Holy Spirit but I have never built my ministry on them, even though I move heavily in them during my meetings. I often have very specific words of knowledge, wisdom, or prophecy for people in my meetings. These are words I know God is speaking to my heart to relay to His people. But even though it's wonderful and many people are blessed by this, it's not what I focus on. That's not my ministry's foundation.

Both my personal and my ministry's foundation are the same— the teachings of Jesus and the rest of Bible! Any word I get that goes against that, well, I just throw it out the door and don't give it a second thought. God's Word is my final authority.

CHAPTER 19

God Speaks Through Dreams

Another way God speaks to His people is through dreams and visions. One time I was sleeping and dreaming that I was preaching! Man, the spit was flying! I was preaching so good that I was "shucking the corn," like we would say in Louisiana.

In my dream, I kept repeating the same phrase over and over again. I kept saying, "When you understand the Word of God, you've got to energize and immobilize and finalize!"

It wasn't as if I was actually preaching, but I was standing on the side and watching myself preach. I kept hearing my voice repeating the words, "Energize! Immobilize! Finalize!"

Suddenly, in the middle of the dream, I woke up and found myself standing in the middle of my bed. The ceiling fan was on low, but it was hitting the top of my hair! My wife, Cathy, woke up just then and saw how close I was to getting my head lopped off. She hollered, "Get down, Jesse!"

Boy, it was a dream from God! In fact, when I woke up I was pointing my index finger to the ceiling and moving it up and down as I preached. God must have been taking care of me, because every time I'd stick my hand up, it would coincide with the ceiling fan blade rotation in just the right way. I'd move my finger up right between the blades and bring it down just in time before it got hit!

Sure enough, it wasn't long after this dream that I found myself in a tent revival preaching, with sweat dripping down the back of my legs and spit flying! In the middle of my sermon, God brought the words to my memory, "When you understand God's word, you'll energize, immobilize, and finalize!" I spoke these words, and out of my spirit came a sermon that was so strong the people were on their feet hollering, "Glory!" and "Hallelujah!"

I began to flow in the spirit, preaching on understanding the Word of God so you can energize yourself to act on it, immobilize the devil's plans for your defeat, and finalize your victory in Jesus!

I didn't plan the sermon. I didn't write the sermon. I didn't research for the sermon. It came right out of my spirit, because it had been deposited there in a God-given dream. It was something that the people needed to hear that night, and God brought it out at the right time. This is a way God speaks to people. He spoke this way to me and I relayed it to His people that night in the tent. What a night!

A Valid Communication

In the Bible, you can research many stories where God used dreams to speak to His people. It's a valid way God talks to us.

In the Old Testament, it was used often as a way for God to communicate with people. In Numbers 12:6, God validated the dream and the vision as a way He communicates when He said, " ...*Hear now my words: If there be a prophet among you, I the Lord will make myself known unto him in a vision, and will speak unto him in a dream.*"

Visions and dreams do tend to go together. God used visions and dreams as a way to communicate in Bible times, but the closer we get to Jesus' returning, the more and more God is going to use this way of communicating with us according to Acts 2:17:

> *"And it shall come to pass in the last days, saith God, I will pour out of my Spirit upon all flesh: and your sons and your daughters shall prophesy, and your young men shall see visions, and your old men shall dream dreams."*

The Story of Joseph

I love the story of Joseph because it shows how far God-given dreams can take a person. In Genesis 37, you can read about young Joseph and his many God-given dreams. His brothers hated him for those dreams. Really, they were just jealous because Joseph was the baby of the family and Dad's favorite son.

Baby Joseph was born when his dad was already old, and that must have put a soft spot in the old man's heart for Joseph. The Bible makes it clear that this boy was the favorite, and one day Daddy shows his love by giving Joe a colorful coat. This ticks off Joe's brothers. They already knew Daddy loved Joe more than the rest of them, and the Bible tells us that after the coat was given they just couldn't talk peaceably to their little brother! I imagine that every time these boys looked at that coat, they felt pangs of jealousy.

You've probably heard the story of Joseph and his coat of many colors before. But his life was about so much more than that little coat. Here's my paraphrase of what happened in the life of this great, dreamer of God-given dreams. You can read the stories for yourself in Genesis 37 and 38.

Joseph's brothers hated him for all his great, lofty dreams because, you see, he didn't just dream—he talked about his dreams. And Joseph didn't have ordinary dreams. He had dreams of greatness that were so much larger than his circumstances. Take this one for instance. Joe dreamt that his mother, father, and brothers were bowing down to him. When he told them, they said, "What's the matter with you? Do you really think you're going to have some kind of control over us?!" They were furious! After all, this was the younger one talking to the older ones.

Joe had another one that the sun, moon, and eleven stars bowed down to him. When he told this to his dad, his dad interpreted it in the-same way as the other dream and said, "Do you really think your mother and me and your brothers are going to bow down to you?" But-it did weigh on the dad's mind. He must have known his son wasn't having ordinary dreams for the Scripture to record that he was mindful of it.

The story goes that these proud brothers were out of town feeding their flock without Joseph. I'm sure they were happy to be away from the dreamer for a little while. But Dad sends Joe to catch up with his brothers and when they see him coming from far off, they start talking murder. They're tired of this dreaming thing.

They start saying, "Hey, let's kill him, throw him in some pit, and tell Dad that some wild animal got him. We'll see what becomes of his big dreams!" Not only were they were conspiring to murder, but they were mocking Joseph's God-given dreams.

God steps in.

Reuben hears the brothers talking at just the right time and butts in on the conversation by saying, "Look boys, don't kill him. Just throw him in a hole." Rueben is thinking he'll save Joseph once they leave and bring him back to his dad. Meanwhile, Joseph is still walking closer. Just as he gets near them, the brothers grab him, strip him of his coat of many colors, and dump him in a nearby pit. Reuben goes back to whatever he's doing, thinking he'll come by later and get the boy.

Around mealtime, the brothers sit down in the field and begin eating bread and talking, while their brother in the pit doesn't have so much as a cup of water to drink. While they're eating, they notice a bunch of Ishmeelites coming by who are heading down to Egypt with spices and perfume. One of the brothers speaks up, "Hey, let's sell Joe, not kill him. After all, he is our flesh and blood. This way we won't have blood on our hands." They were obviously still contemplating killing Joseph.

The brothers agreed to sell him and sold Joseph to the Ishmeelites for twenty shekels of silver. Then, they dipped that colorful coat in blood and told their father Joseph had been killed and eaten by an "evil beast."

Not knowing what conspired, Reuben comes by and sees the boy isn't in the hole and tears his coat because he's so sad. He thinks Joe is dead.

Life in Egypt

Meanwhile, Joseph is on the way to Egypt. But God is with this boy. It isn't too long before he's sold to a captain of the guard and an officer of Pharaoh, named Potiphar. This is a high-ranking official Joseph is slaving for.

Potiphar was a wise man, and he noticed that every project he gave Joseph got done and whatever he put in Joseph's hand prospered. That's because God had His hand on the boy. But the man's wife messed things up by accusing him of sexual harassment, which he

WANTING A GOD YOU CAN TALK TO

didn't do, and that got him thrown in prison. This could have been the end of him, but it wasn't.

God wasn't finished with Joseph yet. Even in prison He uses Joseph. In this prison, Joseph interprets dreams for two palace workers who were thrown into prison—the butler and the baker. Joseph hears the butler's dream and interprets it, and I'll paraphrase the interpretation. Joe says, "Butler, you're going back to work. But the baker's gonna get the ax and his head is going to be hanging from a tree three days from now." It happened, but once the butler was released and given back his job, he forgot about Joseph.

For two years Joseph was in prison, still for that unjust sexual harassment charge. But after these long two years, a person of high importance starts having nightmares. Who is it? It's Pharaoh!

The nightmares were ruining Pharaoh's mood. He called for all his palace magicians and wise men, but nobody knew what the bad dreams meant. So, what happens? The butler gets his memory back! He remembers Joseph's dream interpretations from his days in the big house, and before you know it, Joseph is in the palace telling the meaning of Pharaoh's bad dreams. Seven years of good times were in store, but after that, famine is coming to the land according to the dreams—seven long years of it.

When Interpretation Turns to Advice

Then Joseph goes further. He decides not only to interpret Pharaoh's dream, but also to give advice based on the interpretation. He tells Pharaoh a plan of action to avoid everyone starving during the famine years. The plan? Joseph says, "Appoint officers over the land to collect one-fifth of the produce of grain during the years of plenty, store it under your authority, and keep the food in the cities.

186

Then there will be a reserve for the famine and nobody will starve." The exact quote of the dream and interpretation can be found in Genesis 41:1-37.

Now, Pharaoh recognizes that Joseph is a man "...*in whom the Spirit of God is*" and accepts the advice as wise counsel from a wise and godly man. (Genesis 41:38.) Next, Pharaoh starts wondering who he could hire to oversee this big food saving project.

His solution?

Joseph, the prisoner!

Here's what the Scriptures say:

"And Pharaoh said unto Joseph, Forasmuch as God hath shewed thee all this, there is none so discreet and wise as thou art:

"Thou shalt be over my house, and according unto thy word shall all my people be ruled: only in the throne will I be greater than thou.

"And Pharaoh said unto Joseph, See, I have set thee over all the land of Egypt.

"And Pharaoh took off his ring from his hand, and put it upon Joseph's hand, and arrayed him in vestures of fine linen, and put a gold chain about his neck;

"And he made him to ride in the second chariot which he had; and they cried before him, Bow the knee: and he made him ruler over all the land of Egypt.

"And Pharaoh said unto Joseph, I am Pharaoh, and without thee shall no man lift up his hand or foot in all the land of Egypt.

"And Pharaoh called Joseph's name Zaphnath-pa'aneah; and he gave him to wife Asenath the daughter of Potipherah priest of On. And Joseph went out over all the land of Egypt.

"And Joseph was thirty years old when he stood before Pharaoh king of Egypt. And Joseph went out from the presence of Pharaoh, and went throughout all the land of Egypt."

Genesis 41:39-46

God-given dreams are powerful ways God communicates. In Joseph's life, his ability to hear and understand God's way of communicating, brought him before Pharaoh and made him into a great leader—overnight. From the prison to the palace! It's a wonderful story of a life affected by this amazing way God communicates with His people.

Dreams, Dreams, and More Dreams

There is a difference, of course, in normal dreams and in God-given dreams. In your spirit, you wake up and know the difference. Spiritual dreams just won't leave you alone. They nag at your spirit, not just your mind, and they want to be listened to and often acted upon. They come out of your spirit at opportune times and allow you to help others or yourself.

God spoke to many people in biblical times through dreams. In the Old Testament, He spoke to Abimelech about Sarah being Abraham's wife. (Genesis 20:3.) He spoke to Jacob through his dream of the ladder to Heaven, the ring-straked cattle and of going down into Egypt. (Genesis 28:12, 31:10-13, 46:3.) He spoke to Laban about Jacob. (Genesis 31:24.) He spoke to Solomon concerning wisdom.

(1 Kings 3:3-15.) He spoke to Daniel about the four beasts and the far-off future, even into the end times that we live in today. (Daniel 7.)

And in the New Testament, God didn't stop talking to His children through dreams. Although there is more dream-talk in the Old Testament, dreams are still spoken of in the New Testament.

It was how God spoke to Joseph, Jesus' earthly father. He first spoke to Joseph through a dream about the reality of Mary's virgin birth. He spoke to Joseph about leaving and going to Egypt with Mary and returning to Israel.

You don't hear too much about dreams during Jesus' life, because Jesus was on the earth. He was right here, talking to us face to face! There wasn't much need for dreams at that point! It wasn't until Jesus was captured and it was being decided who would be crucified and who would be let go—Jesus or Barabbas—that a dream is mentioned. And it's Pilate's wife who speaks up to tell her husband while he's sitting in the judgment seat, *"...Have thou nothing to do with that just man: for I have suffered many things this day in a dream because of him"* (Matthew 27:19).

That dream was God's way of speaking to the wife of the man who would pass judgment, that indeed Jesus was a just man. He-was completely blameless and yet being sentenced to be nailed to a cross.

After Jesus' death, visions begin to be more written of in the Bible than dreams. Cornelius has a vision concerning Peter. (Acts 10:3-6.) Peter has a vision of the ceremonially unclean creatures. (Acts 10:10-16.) Paul has a vision in Acts 16:9 of a Macedonian man who says, "Come over into Macedonia and help us!"

This doesn't mean God stopped giving dreams because He didn't, and He will continue to use this method. As I quoted before, even until the end of time, God will use dreams as a form of communication with man.

> *"And it shall come to pass in the last days, saith God, I will pour out of my Spirit upon all flesh: and your sons and your daughters shall prophesy, and your young men shall see visions, and your old men shall dream dreams."*

Acts 2:17

CHAPTER 20

God Speaks Through Visions

In my opinion, it takes more faith or intimacy with God to have a vision than it does to have a dream from God. Why do I think this? Because (1) visions are given when you are in a conscious state and (2) dreams are given while you're in an unconscious state.

When God gives you a dream, there isn't a mental struggle to get you to pay attention or listen to what He is saying to you. But a vision is a totally different thing! God has to somehow get your mind off the natural circumstances that are going on around you. And that can be tough!

I believe that sometimes God can't get people's attention while their awake, so He uses the stillness of sleep to speak to us through dreams. Sometimes, that's the only time some people will listen. Now, that's just my opinion and you can just dismiss it if you don't agree.

Visions come in the conscious state of mind. You can be playing music with the praise and worship team at church and *wham!* A vision starts happening. Now, your fingers are still playing the instrument, your mouth is still singing the song, but you are tuned in to something else. All of a sudden you are seeing something from God. God is using pictures to speak to you. This is one way He communicates.

You could be in your bedroom, praying and worshiping God. The anointing falls and *wham!* A vision begins. You are no longer just in your bedroom, but you are seeing beyond those walls, seeing what God wants you to see.

A Personal Vision,

Now, I have had many visions, but I guess one of the visions that sticks out in my mind the most happened while I was staying at a pastor's home in the early years of my ministry. It wasn't biblical and didn't hold any significance for my preaching. It was personal, something God wanted me to see and to share with my family.

Now, during the early years of my ministry, times were tough when it came to finances. I would preach and sometimes get no offering.

Nothing.

Not fifty-cents, not a quarter—nothing! It was tough.

Pastors would call me up and say, "Listen, I want you to preach for my church, but we don't have much so I can't promise you anything." I'd preach five days straight and get just was I was promised, nothing. Even though I was thrilled to do it, I am still a human and I needed to eat!

There were many forced fasts in the beginning of my ministry. I never stayed in a hotel back then, because I had no money to stay in a hotel. I'd sleep on army cots in Sunday school rooms, unless of course the pastor allowed me to stay in his home. Then I'd stay there.

So after this morning service, instead of going to a hotel, the pastor said, "Why don't you come back to my house? I have a little guest bedroom and you can just lie down an hour or so before the service if you would like to rest your body."

I said, "Yeah, I think I would."

So I go into this room, and man, it was little. I am talking about little! You could sit down, put your feet out, and hit the wall at the same time. I mean, this is a small room. There was no such thing as a double bed in this room. You could fit a single bed and that was it.

The pastor had this giant, white dog that would come right up to you and just breathe his hot, stinky dog breath on you. He was like the house's portable heater. His breath would heat up a room with stink. I'm telling you, that dog's breath would make you sweat!

When the dog tried to share living quarters with me, I thought, *Oh no. This ain't gonna happen today.* So I said, "Dog, get out." The dog wouldn't leave. He'd just sit there breathing on me.

This dog was kind of a cool dog. He would carry his food bowl around with him from room to room. He would just pick it up, come and sit by you, and just snack all day. I'd try and reach for his bowl and he would growl, which meant, "Do you want to draw back a nub, boy?" I was always trying to get his food bowl. For some reason, I like making dogs growl. I just think it's funny.

The pastor had a cat too, and the cat would casually walk by just in time to meet that big dog's tail face to face. *Whap!* The dog's tail would hit the cat, and the cat would be eating carpet for a second or two. It was a regular circus with these two around. And all I wanted was to rest my body and prepare for the next service.

So I got the dog out and quickly shut the door so the dog couldn't come in and breathe on me. I sat down on the bed, leaned over to take my shoes off, and *whoosh!* All of a sudden, I was not in that room anymore. I was beginning a vision from God. Now, my mind wasn't on having a vision. I had just preached and my mind was on resting, getting away from the animals, and reading the Word.

But suddenly, I was on clouds. I saw my Aunt Elsie Mae, who had passed away two months before that. I was having a vision and I didn't even really realize what was going on. I looked and my Aunt was far, far away and talking to me. She was saying, "Jesse, Jesse, Jesse!" Surprised and happy to see her, I said to myself, "Hey! That is Aunt Elsie!"

I looked at her and hollered back, "Hey! Hey!" I'd been to her funeral two months before, and honestly, no one really knew if she was saved. She was waving at me and had her hands cupped around her mouth hollering out at me, "Tell them I made it! Tell them I made it!" I began to talk back, "Hey! Say hello to————," but I stopped because then I saw my grandfather walking behind Aunt Elsie Mae. And then, I saw his daughter walking behind him towards me too.

Now, I loved my grandfather, but he died when I was only eleven years old. He was a huge man and I am the smallest one in my family. My memories of him are really good. He was so big, he wore a size fifteen ring! I remember him picking me up with one hand and raising me in the air to pick oranges off a tree. The man had fingers like sausages and he called me "little Jesse." I just loved him so much.

My mother had gotten him to say the sinner's prayer only seven days before he died. His name was Gillis Este, pronounced the Cajun French way.

I saw my grandfather walk up and put his arm around my Aunt Elsie, who had just passed. I said to myself, "That is Papa!" I hollered, "Hey Papa!"

He said, "How are you doing, little Jesse?"

I was so shocked to be seeing all of this, that there wasn't much I could say. So, I just kept excitedly saying, "Hey!" to everyone. I was so excited. Boy, I loved my grandfather and it was so good to see him after so many years. His daughter didn't speak but just stood on the side by my Aunt Elsie Mae.

Then, suddenly I saw another man come up and stand behind my grandfather. He had white hair like mine. He even combed it the same way I do! He looked at me and he proudly said, "You look good."

I said, "Thank you. Who are you?" I didn't recognize his face. I'd never seen this man before.

But all he said was, "You look good."

"Thank you," I said. And, I thought to myself, *I don't know who this dude is. Who is this guy?*

I was just looking at my grandpa and my Aunt Elsie and all of a sudden, I was back leaning over with my hand on my shoes. I thought to myself, *What is happening?*

What happened? I'd just had a vision. God had wanted me to know something, so He chose to speak to me with a vision.

Well, I finished that night's service and drove home. About two weeks later, my favorite uncle, Uncle Ray, came over to my house. Uncle Ray is my mother's brother.

Telling the Vision

It was morning, and Cathy cooked a little breakfast for us. I knew I had to share what I'd seen with him. So I said, "Uncle Ray, I want to tell you something. Now, this is going to sound nuts, but I just want you to know."

He looked at me for a second. "What, Jesse?"

"I saw Aunt Elsie."

Now, this is his sister I was talking about. There were eight children in my mother's family. There were four sisters and four brothers, one of which was my Uncle Ray.

He said, "What?!"

"Uncle Ray,." I said, "I know it sounds nuts but..." and I went through the whole story. From the dogs to the cat, to bending over to undo my shoes, and *boom!* Clouds, Aunt Elsie, Grandpa, his daughter, some old man I didn't know—the whole thing.

"Uncle Ray," I said, "Aunt Elsie was hollering..."

"Hollering, what do you mean?"

"She was hollering. She had her hands cupped to her mouth and she was far off and saying, 'Tell them I made it'!"

And when I said that last thing, my Uncle Ray busted out in tears.

I didn't know it, but he had been praying, "Oh God, did my sister make Heaven her home?" He'd been thinking, *God, she was a wonderful person, and a real blessing. But I just didn't know if she was truly saved or born again in her heart.*

That vision God showed me of Aunt Elsie gave my Uncle Ray such comfort and peace. When I told him I'd seen Grandpa, Uncle Ray said, "You saw Daddy?" My grandpa was his dad.

"Yeah, I did."

My Uncle Raymond's face looked like wood. It was a heavy-duty vision, and I could see that he was trying to absorb everything I was saying.

"But there was some white headed dude, Uncle Ray," I went on, "a guy that had hair like me, you know? He just came up and I don't know who he was. And he said this, 'You look good.'"

Uncle Ray didn't know who I was talking about, so we decided to get out the family photo album. Man, I had some poor relatives. It's funny how when you look back at old pictures, it seems like everybody was leaning against or hanging off the side of a barn door.

All the pictures were black and white, and I've never seen one wealthy relative in a photo. It's always some guy hanging onto a shovel, or next to a mule, his pants half hanging on, wearing no belt, busted shoes, and a hat cocked sideways. I have pictures of people I don't even know. They're old, wrinkled up, black-and-white photos that I inherited when my mama died.

So Uncle Ray and I are looking through the photo album, and he starts telling me the names of all the people I don't know. I'd point out some crusty old woman and he'd say, "That's your great, great aunt that died of pneumonia when she was eighty-nine years old." It wasn't too impressive since they all looked miserable and poor.

Well, we're just going along down his memory lane through our family history, and he pulls out this picture of a man. To tell you the truth, I had never even seen the picture before, or if I did, I don't remember seeing it. The man had white hair that was parted down the middle like mine. Uncle Ray said, "Jesse, is this the man you saw?"

I looked at the picture and knew immediately it was the same man. "Yeah, that is the guy. That is him, man! That's the dude. Who is that?"

"That is your great-grandfather, Grandpa Arceneaux. He's my grandpa. He was the first person to ever get saved in this family, and it is because of him that all of us are saved today."

I was so shocked.

"Jesse," Uncle Ray said, "look, he had hair just like you. It was white and he combed it like you do. You know what, Jesse? Grandpa Arceneaux saw you born, and he died two weeks after that. I remember him holding you about three or four days before he died, and he kept saying, 'He looks good.'"

"You heard him say that?"

"Yeah, I heard him say that to your mama. He'd say, 'Your boy looks good. He looks good.'"

I was just sitting there, looking at the photo, taking it all in. I was calculating the time in my head for some reason, thinking to myself, *If I was born July 9, 1949, and he died two weeks later, that means he was looking at me on July 12th or 13th and by the 23rd he passed on. Now he sees me as a man and says the same thing, 'Hey, you look good.' Wow!*

I never saw him, but he saw me. And God must have wanted me to see my Grandpa Arceneaux during my lifetime. So, I saw him in a vision. I often wondered why I didn't see others, why God wouldn't show me everyone like my mother and my grandmother. But now that I think of it, there was no question in my mind or my family's mind of where they went. We knew they went to Heaven!

My uncle's heart was heavy for his sister because of the uncertainty of her salvation. God put him at ease through the vision. I lost my grandpa when I was young and missed him and God assured me I'd see him soon again through the vision. And why he showed me my Grandpa Arceneaux, I don't know. But it blessed me just the same, and I'm appreciative of the opportunity to see the man who received salvation first in our family.

Bible Visions

Stories of people having visions are throughout the Bible and there are all sorts of reasons why God may use this way to communicate.

In Genesis 15:1-16, you can read about Abraham's vision from God:

> *"After these things the word of the LORD came unto Abram in a vision, saying, Fear not, Abram: I am thy shield, and thy exceeding great reward.*
>
> *"And Abram said, Lord GOD, what wilt thou give me, seeing I go childless, and the steward of my house is this Eliezer of Damascus?*
>
> *"And Abram said, Behold, to me thou hast given no seed: and, lo, one born in my house is mine heir.*
>
> *"And, behold, the word of the LORD came unto him, saying, This shall not be thine heir; but he that shall come forth out of thine own bowels shall be thine heir.*
>
> *"And he brought him forth abroad, and said, Look now toward heaven, and tell the stars, if thou be able to number them: and he said unto him, So shall thy seed be"* (vv.1-5).

As an old man, Abraham had this vision. But God made it come to pass, and Abraham and his wife Sara eventually had Isaac, whose descendents were David, and later Jesus Christ Himself! And through Jesus, we are all adopted sons and daughters of God. So Abraham's physical seed was great, but his spiritual seed was even greater because of everyone who has accepted Jesus as Lord and Savior.

This vision recorded in Genesis was not only a great encouragement to a childless old man, but it is also a comfort to all who read it and realize that they are seeds of this great man of faith—and heirs to his great blessings. That's why he is called Father Abraham.

Now, that's a vision that happened way back in Genesis. And there are visions recorded all through the Bible. In the book of Revelation, however, there are some of the greatest visions ever recorded. In that book of the Bible, the apostle John describes his visions during the days he spent in exile on the island of Patmos. This-book of the Bible contains a series of prophetic visions. There is a lot of symbolism, numbers, and imagery in this book to describe what is going to happen in the future; and that's common with visions from God.

A vision is like a movie playing spiritual concepts. You see it with your eyes and try to process the information with your mind. But the mind doesn't really get it. This is what 1 Corinthians 2:14 means when it says, *"But the natural man receiveth not the things of the Spirit of God: for they are foolishness unto him: neither can he know them, because they are spiritually discerned."*

That's why visions and dreams often need interpretation from someone who can spiritually discern the things of God. Some people in Bible times had visions and knew exactly what they meant because they had spiritually discerned it.

Others who had dreams or visions didn't understand what they'd seen. They needed someone to help them out, just like the story I shared earlier about Joseph and Pharaoh. John's book of Revelation contains his description of the deep prophetic visions God gave him. I don't believe that God would have bothered keeping the book in the

Bible if it wasn't important that we read it and understand some of what it's saying.

Today we are blessed to have those who have studied the book of Revelation and believe they are able to spiritually discern what the visions describe. They're teachers on end times. It's their specialty, so to speak. As an evangelist, my specialty is stirring people up about God and introducing them to His Son, Jesus. I also like spreading the joy of the Lord because it's a sad world out there. The message of Jesus is Good News, not bad news. So I'm happy to tell it!

Visions are a wonderful way God communicates. Now, let's move on to another way God speaks to His kids.

CHAPTER 21

God Speaks Through the Gift of Tongues

Another way God speaks to His children is through the gift of tongues. I know this is a controversial subject and some people don't believe in it. I do! Just like they have a right not to believe, I've got a right to believe. Don't you just love God's system of free will? There's nothing like it.

When I want to preach on the Holy Spirit, I just preach Jesus' message about the Holy Ghost and power because I figure that when a person gets ready and when they choose to reach out for more of God's presence, something dramatic will happen in their life. If they want it, that Holy Spirit that is living in them will bubble up, fill them up, and overflow! They'll be filled to overflowing with His fiery presence!

Now, tongues isn't just a bunch of babbling. It might sound that way, but it isn't. It's a gift of the Holy Spirit and it has a couple of functions: (1) tongues for your personal edification, and (2) tongues for everybody's edification!

Tongues for Personal Edification

Now, remember that the Holy Spirit is that part of God that comes inside you when you invite Jesus into your heart. But, the baptism of the Holy Spirit happens when you actively reach out to God with a heartfelt request to have more of Him. When that is the sincere desire of your heart and you request it, God's Holy Spirit rises up within you so much that it spills out! With that spillage comes the blessing of a new prayer language.

Jesus prophesied that speaking in tongues would be a sign of the Holy Ghost's presence. *"And these signs shall follow them that believe; In my name shall they cast out devils; they shall speak with new tongues"*(Mark 16:17).

Paul said it was a sign too in 1 Corinthians 14:22. Peter also taught that speaking in tongues is a sign of the indwelling of the Holy Spirit. His teaching can be studied in Acts 10:44-46, 11:16-17, and 15:7-9.

The ability to speak in tongues is what many people call the "evidence" of having been baptized in the Spirit. The word *baptism* translates "to dunk," so that's a good way to think about it. When you're dunked with the Holy Spirit, it's like being dunked—but from the inside out! It comes from inside and flows right out of your mouth. Suddenly, you start saying combinations of syllables you've never spoken before. It's as if God takes over your tongue!

Now, the Holy Spirit of God is alive with power and that power rises up within you. What's it for? To witness for Jesus, of course. That's the whole message of Christianity. Tongues help you be a better witness because they give you boldness. Acts 1:8 confirms, *"But ye shall receive power, after that the Holy Ghost is come upon you: and ye shall be witnesses unto me both in Jerusalem, and in all Judaea, and in Samaria, and unto the uttermost part of the earth."*

Personal tongues are for your personal edification and are meant to help you as you pray. You use them as you feel led to, whenever you're moved by the Lord to do so. This is a language that you can use every day and it's a way of praying that you just can't mess up! Speaking in tongues is a real benefit to being born again because God can use you to pray for things you wouldn't normally think about. Although this prayer language is private, people pray in tongues in church during prayer times, or praise and worship service. It's a way for a group to pray corporately.

But personal tongues aren't something you go around shouting out in church when it's quiet or when the minister is preaching! It just-wouldn't profit anyone else for you to do that. And you could get thrown out if you disrupt the service like that! 1 Corinthians 14:2 says, *"For he that speaketh in an unknown tongue speaketh not unto men, but unto God: for no man understandeth him; howbeit in the spirit he speaketh mysteries."* This kind of tongues is a private way of-praying from your spirit and it's not for the spotlight.

Speaking in an unknown tongue isn't an Old Testament gift. It started after Jesus went to the cross and sent His Holy Spirit. It first happened on the Day of Pentecost and it's a gift from God to His kids to help them pray easier, to be more effective and bold to witness for Christ.

When Tongues Go Public

There is another function of the gift of tongues and it's one distinct way God speaks to His people. Sometimes tongues go public!

Sometimes the Holy Spirit moves upon an individual to deliver a specific word in the form of tongues to a group of people.

This public exhortation in an unknown tongue is like a word of knowledge, wisdom, or prophecy, in that it's a specific message from God. But during this time, the message is for the public and not just one person. Many times the tongue message is shouted out in church!

It's what some call "prophesying" and although it is first delivered in tongues, it is for everyone. If it's a message from God, you will notice that everyone falls silent as the person loudly speaks the message in tongues. Everybody gets quiet because inside their spirit, they know they are hearing a message from God. You may have seen this happen before. It's a real phenomenon of the New Testament church that's been happening since the Day of Pentecost.

What happens is that everyone recognizes God's chain of command. The spirit of a person knows when God is talking and shuts up to listen! During a public exhortation using tongues, it's as if God is saying, "I have a message for this church." The Holy Spirit within a person in the congregation rises up, and suddenly, that individual knows he has a message from God.

It is interesting that everyone in the church gets so quiet. People want to hear God talk! After the message in tongues is delivered, people will still be quiet for a while. No one will usually praise or shout. Why? Because the message hasn't yet been fully delivered! It is in need of interpretation!

During this short downtime, or the time between the tongues and the interpretation, everybody remains in a state of quiet prayer. This is very important. It shows you are being respectful of the Holy Spirit and it gives the interpreter a bit of time to obey the prompting he or she is getting from the Holy Spirit.

Interpretation of Tongues

The interpretation of tongues is also a gift of the Spirit. This gift allows someone to supernaturally reveal the meaning of the message in tongues. The interpreter doesn't understand the tongue he is interpreting. It's not like he hears it and as it is being delivered he understands every word and decides to translate it. It's not that kind of natural interpretation.

It's a supernatural interpretation, not a natural translation. So, as the person hears the message in tongues, he or she is just like everybody else—without understanding but respectful of God's message and prayerful concerning the interpretation.

The interpreter's job is to flow in the gift of the Spirit by simply proclaiming whatever meaning is in the message. This is a supernatural thing! It's powerful to watch for the first time and it never ceases to amaze me how God uses this way to talk!

God wants His people to understand the message, so the interpretation will always be delivered in whatever the common language of the group is. If the message is delivered in an English speaking church, the interpretation will come in English. If the message is delivered in a Chinese speaking church, the interpretation will be in Chinese.

If there is no interpretation, a public message in tongues doesn't help anybody. Why? Because nobody can understand it! And what good is it if nobody understands the message?

Also, the interpretation usually comes from someone else in the group. It's as if God wants to give somebody else a chance to participate in relaying His message. Some people ask, "How do you know if you're supposed to give a message in tongues?" Or,

"How do you know if you're the one who is supposed to deliver the interpretation?"

A person knows because in his or her spirit there is an intense urging to deliver the message. It's so strong that they simply can't contain it. They absolutely know in their spirit, not in their mind, that they have something from God to say. Their mind may question them and throw fear of humiliation at them, but the person knows in their heart that the message must be heard. It has to be heard. There is no other choice in the matter.

That urging is the Holy Spirit within them that continually nags at them until they do it. If they obey Him, the message in tongues almost erupts out of their mouth. And like I mentioned before, everyone will get quiet to hear it.

If they don't obey, because they're too embarrassed or they just wait too long contemplating whether they should deliver it or not, the Holy Spirit will give the message to another person in the group. This is how it works. God wants His message heard. If a person isn't willing to deliver what He is giving them, to just trust Him and begin speaking, then the Holy Spirit will move on to someone who will obey Him. It starts with your obedience and faith.

When you know you have an interpretation, you begin speaking in faith and God gives you the words. He often doesn't give the whole message to you. You often only know one sentence or maybe a few words at a time. He requires that you trust Him to use your mouth and not rely on anything else but Him during this time. That's how you don't mess the message up! You leave your mind out of it and just let the words flow from your spirit. After all, you're just relaying the message; you're not making the message.

The supernatural combination of the gift of tongues and interpretation of tongues is a powerful way God speaks to us.

Don't Mix It Up

In the early church things got out of hand and Paul had to set some guidelines down. People were so excited about having a new Heavenly way of praying that they would all pray in tongues at once, as if each one of their personal prayers in tongues was a message for the entire group.

It wasn't.

Personal tongues have nothing to do with public exhortation.

A lot of beleivers were simply praying in their personal tongues. So, it didn't do anyone else in the church any good. They had to grow and mature to learn how to use this great gift from God, which is what these verses in 1 Corinthians are all about:

"But he that prophesieth speaketh unto men to edification, and exhortation, and comfort.

"He that speaketh in an unknown tongue edifieth himself; but he that prophesieth edifieth the church.

"I would that ye all spake with tongues, but rather that ye prophesied: for greater is he that prophesieth than he that speaketh with tongues, except he interpret, that the church may receive edifying."

1 Corinthians 14:3-5

The word "edifying" means that the message should be instructive and encouraging, helping you to improve as a believer. God doesn't condemn people. He brings conviction to their hearts to improve in a strong but loving way. He doesn't beat people up. He loves people and guides them through encouraging and instructive words. When

God has a message for a group of people, it won't come out as overly anxious, awkward, or constrained.

First Corinthians 14:26 says, *"How is it then, brethren? when ye come together, every one of you hath a psalm, hath a doctrine, hath a tongue, hath a revelation, hath an interpretation. Let all things be done unto edifying."*

First Corinthians 14:40 commands us, *"Let all things be done decently and in order."*

So, messages in tongues and interpretations that follow shouldn't be chaotic or confused. They'll be decent, orderly, and edifying to everybody.

CHAPTER 22

The Odd Ways God Speaks

God is pretty unusual. In the Scripture, there is even mention that God wants to talk so badly that if we don't communicate with Him, the rocks will start crying out. (Luke 19:37-40.)

God will even go so far as to use lower life forms to speak to us! If He wants to get our attention but can't get through to us any other way, He is not above using a donkey or a dog. He will use a chicken to get your attention. It sounds crazy but it's true. You don't have to believe me but consider this: Peter never repented until that bird said, "Cockle doodle doo!" Think about it!

Matthew 26:34 says, *"Jesus said unto him, Verily I say unto thee, That this night, before the cock crow, thou shalt deny me thrice."*

After Jesus was captured and Peter was roaming around, people began to recognize him as one who followed Jesus. Peter denied it. Then he was asked a second time if he followed Jesus and he denied it.

By the third time someone asked him this, Matthew 26 records Peter doing this: *"Then began he to curse and to swear, saying, I know not the man. And immediately the cock crew"* (v. 74). Do you know what happened then? *"And Peter remembered the word of Jesus, which said unto him, Before the cock crow, thou shalt deny methrice. And he went out, and wept bitterly"*(v. 75).

The boy cried because he knew he'd just denied Jesus. How did he know it? Because the rooster crowed. God used that rooster to prove a point to Peter. The point? Repent! Repent! Repent!

Peter knew that he was wrong. He knew that he had betrayed Jesus by denying Him. Really, he did the same thing Judas did. Except Judas couldn't accept forgiveness. He thought his sin was too big to be forgiven. Peter understood grace and went on to do great things for God.

The point I'm trying to make is that God will use animals and lower forms of life to get your attention if you are not listening to Him.

Once there was a prophet coming to town and he was riding this donkey. Suddenly, his donkey slammed him up against a wall. It made the prophet mad! The whole story is in Numbers 22:21-35, but I'll paraphrase it:

He said, "I am going to kill you!"

And that donkey said, "What do you want to kill me for? I am trying to save your life!"

The most amazing thing to me about the story is that the prophet is actually talking back to the donkey! I mean, he's got a Mr. Ed donkey and he doesn't seem fazed by it. The donkey is talking back to him!

The man says, "I will kill you if you mess with me, donkey! I can't believe you busted up my leg!"

What happened? That donkey saw the angel of God standing there with a sword and said, "Look, Jack, I am saving your life!"

This is a paraphrase of the story of Balaam and his donkey from Numbers 22. Now, think about the fact that God couldn't get Balaam's attention, so he had to use a little burrow's knee-jerk response to seeing an angel in the middle of the road.

Learning from a Dog

Dogs are so funny. I like big dogs, but I'm small. Do you ever notice that big people often like little bitty dogs? You can be walking down the street and you might see a three-hundred-pound woman holding a little, bitty Chihuahua. Then, you might see a woman who is barely five-feet tall and weighs no more than ninety-eight pounds, and she'll be walking a giant, drooling Saint Bernard! It seems mixed up to me. Big people ought to have big dogs and little people ought to have little dogs.

Anyway, it seems like all my wife and kid ever wanted was a little dog. So, we got one from my uncle and my aunt. It was a poodle, a boy, and my wife named the thing Beau Jacque. My uncle and aunt liked little dogs too, and one time they had a little Pekinese dog. I went over to their house one day and said, "Hey, where's the dog?"

My uncle said, "Oh, Jesse, he died."

"How'd that happen?"

"Two hundred pounds fell on him."

"What?" I said, "What happened?"

He said, "Your aunt fell on him. Killed him. He's dead as a doornail."

I laughed. I knew I shouldn't have but it just sounded so funny. I said, "Well, I guess that's a good way to go. Two hundred pounds jump on you and you're dead pretty quick." My uncle got in so much trouble for telling me that!

This is the home our dog, Beau Jacque, came from. So I figured we saved his life somehow and he ought to be grateful. He wasn't. The dog irritated me. He was really little and white, and had the backbone of a noodle. It was a boy dog but my wife would paint his toenails and put bows on his ears anyway. He hated it. He'd try and scratch off the paint on the sidewalk and rip out his bows. I didn't like the dog too much.

And this dog and I had many conversations about a lot of different things—mostly the problems I had with his things. But, the Lord used that dog one day to teach me a lesson about being quick to listen to His voice.

I was watching television and the Lord said, "Cut the television off and watch Beau Jacque."

I said, "What?"

He said, "Watch Beau Jacque; watch the dog."

So, I cut off the TV and I said, "Beau Jacque."

You know they hear you because they look at you with their little eyes like, What? What? What is he saying? I wish I knew human! What are you saying to me, oh most loved master of the house?

I said, "I am going to watch you."

His big fluffy ears went back. So, I just sat there and watched him. He laid down on the carpet. Nothing was going on. It was silent in the house. Then, all of a sudden, Beau Jacque jumped up and ran to the door. He started growling loudly and scratching at the door.

I am going, "What, God? What? What?"

He said, "Do you notice how his antenna was up? Did you notice how he charged for the object he heard?"

I said, "Yeah."

He said, "Why don't you act like your dog?"

Whoa, God! I thought to myself. He talks to me pretty straightforward sometimes.

He said, "Learn something from that dog."

"The dog ain't even saved, God."

"Learn something. Notice how quick the dog is. He is quick to move when he hears." He said, "I want you to move like that when I speak to you."

Sure enough, somebody had driven up into the driveway. It was my sister-in-law, Deborah. He saw her, turned around, and walked off. But that day God showed me through the example of my dog how important it is to quickly respond to His voice.

Not long after that lesson, I was sleeping in a hotel bedroom and I was sleeping really good. Suddenly, I heard God say, "Jesse" and before I could think, I was up out of the bed. *Bam!* I fell down on the floor. I got up so fast I didn't give time for my blood to work into my legs right. They just wouldn't hold me up!

I thought I had been knocked out in the power of the Spirit. Then it dawned on me, *You idiot, you jumped up too fast.* And the Lord kidded me, "That is a good way to start! I want you to move, be sensitive. When I talk I want you to listen." I thought it was so funny, I got back in bed and God talked to me for a little while and then I fell back off to sleep.

God Speaks Through Nature

God will use His creation to teach you something if you'll listen. I remember this one time that God woke me up at about six-thirty in the morning. He spoke quietly to my spirit and said, "I want you to go to your patio."

Back then I lived in this house that had a large patio attached to the back. It was actually an "L" shaped house originally. But, the previous owners had made it into a square shaped house by creating a large, screened-in patio. I really liked it. I put a picnic table, a swing, and some redwood outdoor furniture out there. Cathy had a lot of plants growing in pots there. It was a real pretty and comfortable place to be, and Cathy and I would go and just sit in our swing in the afternoons.

In fact, for a lot of the year, it was the only place you could go outside and not get eaten up by the giant mosquitoes. If you live in Southern Louisiana, you know that the mosquitoes might as well be the state bird. It's like a million little Draculas flying around in the summer.

Anyway, I got out of bed, went out there to my patio, and sat on my redwood swing. As I sat swinging, I said, "What do you want me to do, Lord?"

"I want you to watch that plant."

"What?"

"Look at that plant over there that Cathy likes so much. The one with the big elephant ears."

"Watch it?"

"Just look at it."

I thought that maybe I was missing something so I said, "You mean, You just want me to sit here and look at that plant?"

"Yeah," He said, "watch it."

So, I thought, *Well, okay.*

As I sat there swinging and watching the plant, I noticed that the sun began to come up and it streamed through the screen on the patio. I watched and the plant began to move very slowly. Now, this is a big plant with big green leaves. I watched it for about thirty minutes and I saw it leaning towards the light.

I said, "Look at that, God! What is it doing?"

He said, "It is leaning towards the light. Now, get up and turn it around."

So I did.

"Now, sit and watch it."

Do you know what happened? That big, leafy plant began to move its leaves back towards the light!

"What are You trying to tell me, God?"

"I am trying to tell you to lean toward the light."

I said, "You mean You got me up to tell me this?"

"Well, if the plant can do it, then why can't you?"

Hummm. He had a point.

Cathy used to talk to that plant. She'd say, "Grow little baby, grow. Mama's coming to feed you today. Grow, grow, grow."

Sometimes I'd pull off a leaf just because I knew it would aggravate Cathy. I'd walk over to the plant and snap! Pop off a leaf. "What do you think of that, plant?" The plant wouldn't say anything, of course. It was probably scared when I walked on the patio, wondering if I was going to pop its leaves off.

But God used that plant to teach me something. I believe that sometimes the little things can teach us great lessons. He created this earth, whether people want to believe it or not, and He uses His creation to teach us principles for living.

Don't Dismiss His Voice

I believe that many people have heard the voice of God and didn't even know it. Perhaps they were like young Samuel, hearing words but thinking they came from someone nearby.

Sometimes you may hear a voice and look around to see who is talking to you. You may dismiss it. And it may just be the audible voice of God. Maybe you thought you heard your grandmother talking to you. Maybe you were driving your car and just heard your grandma say, "I am praying for you, boy." That wasn't your grandma! You just thought it was her voice. In actuality, it was the audible voice of God.

Mikey Hears God's Voice

I'll never forget this child I met named Mikey. I was scheduled to preach a revival for a wonderful pastor friend of mine. That night, before the evening service began, the pastor began letting me know the order of the service and asking me what I'd like to do afterwards.

"Jesse," the pastor said, "we won't be able to go to a restaurant after service because they'll all be closing up at that time. Would you mind coming over to my home? We have set up a meal there in case you want to eat something after service."

"No," I said, "I don't mind that at all. It sounds good to me."

"Listen," he continued, "I have a couple that goes to my church and I would like for you to meet them. I've invited them over to my house too. Would that be okay with you?"

"Yeah, that is fine."

After the service, we drove over to the pastor's house and I met the couple. Now, these were some precious people of God. They had a little boy who blessed my socks off. He was named Mikey and he looked about two and a half years old. I'm not great with age but I will tell you this, I have yet to meet a kid like this again.

When I first saw him, his parents told me his name and I noticed how cute he looked in his little suit. He had blond hair and blue eyes and he was small. They had dressed him like a little man. I greeted him as I would any little child and said, "How are you doing, Mikey?"

"Fine."

He continued, "Brother Jesse, I enjoyed your sermon tonight. It really blessed my spirit and energized my soul." The words were sharp and clear and he looked right at me as he said it.

I just looked at him thinking, *Did I just hear this kid say 'blessed my spirit' and 'energized my soul'?* I could hardly believe it. He kept talking to me.

"It was a blessing from God, Brother Jesse. I can't wait until tomorrow night for tomorrow's sermon."

I don't know if my mouth was hanging open, but if it was, nobody said anything. I thought, *Man, I like this kid!* I looked at his mother and said, "He is brilliant."

"Yes, he is," she said. "We love him. We prayed him here. He is sent by God."

We were all talking before we ate, and the more I was around this little boy, the more amazed I was by him. He was so intelligent for his age. I'm talking brilliant. His speech was like an adult's, even with his parents. But he was so little that they still put him in a high chair.

His words weren't slurred like most kids. They were clear and sharp, and he made complete sentences and used words that only adults would use. It was a treat to see this kind of mind in a little kid.

Soon the food was ready and we were in the dining room. Mikey's mother, who was so proud of her son, was getting him situated in the high chair and she said, "Mikey, would you like to say the blessing over the food?"

Now, I wasn't seated yet and neither was anyone else. The pastor, whose name is Mike, was right beside me and we were all about to take a seat.

"I can't," Mikey says. "Not now, mama. When Pastor Mike finishes talking, then I will pray. But not now."

I looked at the pastor. He hadn't said a word.

All of a sudden Mikey says, "OK! Pastor Mike stopped talking. Everyone bow your heads and let me pray over this food."

Then, the kid started praying. I've heard kids pray and it was nothing like this. Mikey sounded like a little adult as he said in a steady and sincere voice, "Lord, bless this food and sanctify it to our bodies. Minister to us, Lord. Let this meal bring nutritional value to us. In Jesus' name we pray, amen."

I was thinking, *This kid is something!*

Everyone ate and enjoyed the meal.

So, the next night I was preaching at the pastor's church again and I said, "Mike, invite that couple over, will you? Tell them to bring the kid. I want to talk to this kid. This kid is brilliant!"

That night after service, I spoke to the boy. I said, "Mikey, I heard you say last night that you heard Pastor————" but before I could even finish, he closed his eyes and started nodding his head.

"Pastor Mike is speaking again. Oh, that is good! Pastor Mike is standing right by me."

I looked at him and I knew in my heart what was happening with this child. He wasn't hearing Pastor Mike. He was hearing the voice of God, and because Pastor Mike was the person he heard talk about God the most, he put the two together. He thought it was his pastor, when really it was God talking directly to him much the same way He spoke to young Samuel in the Bible.

Samuel thought it was Eli.

Mikey thought it was Pastor Mike.

What Are You Hearing?

Sometimes we hear a voice and we think it's somebody nearby talking to us. But no one hears the voice we hear. In that instance, its audible, but it's only audible to us.

I've heard my mother's and my grandmother's voices before. And they passed away many years ago. I've heard my mother's voice when, in actuality, no one is around. Many people experience this.

Often, that experience is dismissed. Because in today's society they think you're crazy if you hear a voice and nobody is physically standing there. But we are spirit beings, with souls that are encased in a human body. God is a Spirit and that's how He talks to us. There is a spiritual realm that the world pretends doesn't exist. But just because you don't see something, doesn't mean it doesn't exist. That's what faith is all about—believing in something you can't see.

If it doesn't fit into the world's way of thinking, to them it is wrong. But God is mysterious and unusual. Sometimes we hear a voice and mistake it for someone nearby, like little Samuel.

My mother has been dead for a long time now. But I've heard her voice out loud. It's weird. I've thought, *I know that can't be my mother because she's in Heaven having a good time.* But you see, my mother put the Word of God into me as a young boy. Her fingerprint is on that Bible for me! She was my Eli, the one who taught me what the Word said.

Situations come up in my life and I hear the Word quoted to me, sometimes in her voice. I know it's not her. I know that sometimes it's my memory of her quoting it. Nevertheless, if it is the Word of God coming to my remembrance at a crucial time when I need it, then it fits the qualifications Jesus spelled out in John 14:26:

> *"But the Comforter, which is the Holy Ghost, whom the Father will send in my name, he shall teach you all things, and* ***bring all things to your remembrance, whatsoever I have said unto you."***

The Holy Spirit brings the Word back to your memory. The Holy Spirit is God's voice in the earth. So when I hear the word audibly quoted to me and it seems like it's my mother's voice, I know it's the work of the Holy Spirit of God.

God is talking!

I'm listening!

Over the years, many people have told me that they've experienced the same thing. Perhaps they hear their Uncle Fred say something about the Word, but he is across town. Perhaps they heard a voice and didn't know who it was, but thinking they must be crazy to hear a voice, they just dismissed the incident.

I don't mean to say that every voice is God's, because that's just not true. Some people have mental troubles and hear all sorts of stuff! But just because that happens to some people, it doesn't mean we should discount God's ability to speak to us audibly. You don't throw the baby out with the bath water! Don't be afraid to be open to this way that God talks to us.

You just might hear Him calling your name one morning soon.

CHAPTER 23

The Blessing and the Responsibility

Hearing God brings blessing. Proverbs 8:34 says, ***"Blessed is the man that heareth me,*** *watching daily at my gates, waiting at the posts of my doors."*

That Scripture tells us how important it is to hear God, to watch for God, and to wait for God. God has a lot to say. That's why the Bible is so big! He has even more stuff to say to you personally as His child but He will never say something that goes against His Word. Hear, watch, and wait!

A Prayer for Guidance

In my ministry, I have lots of decisions to make. This is a scenario to give you a picture of how my prayers go on those days. That morning, I wake up knowing I have a decision to make, and I run immediately to God's gate and say, "Father, I come boldly to You!"

Jesus Christ meets me at the gate and says, "I'm the High Priest of this place. Nobody gets to God but through Me. I am the Advocate. What do you desire?"

I say, "I've got a giant decision to make for this ministry God's given me, Jesus, and I need some help!"

He says, "Well, let's go before My Father." Jesus and I latch arms, and we start walking to the throne room of God.

I say, "Father, I am here. What should I do about this?" If it were physical, that's how it would look.

But it's not physical; it's spiritual. I am still on this earth, and Jesus is still in Heaven seated at the right hand of the Father. I pray to the Father, in Jesus' name, and the answer is delivered via the Holy Spirit, Who lives inside of me because of my new birth. I get the guidance I need from the "Spirit of truth" as it says in John 16:13-15:

> *"Howbeit when he, the Spirit of truth, is come, he will* **guide you into all truth:** *for he shall not speak of himself; but whatsoever he shall hear, that shall he speak: and he will* **shew you things to come.**
>
> *"He shall glorify me: for he shall receive of mine, and shall shew it unto you.*
>
> **"All things that the Father hath are mine: therefore said I, that he shall take of mine, and shall shew it unto you."**

God is showing Jesus what I should do. Then Jesus is showing the Holy Spirit what I should do. Then the Holy Spirit is showing me what I should do. That's the chain of command God put in place. I don't question it. I simply use it.

That is how you get the mind of Christ on something.

God has given me the mind of Christ, and if you are born again then you've got the mind of Christ too. It may not be developed like Jesus' is, but bless God, if you're praying, you're on your way!

The presence of God isn't some elusive thing. Because of the power of the Holy Spirit, you're made close to God in an instant. You're at His gates in an instant. As soon as that door opens, and it's always open to us because we're blood-bought New Testament kids, you're in there having an audience with God.

You become one blessed kid when you've got God on your side, Jesus as your mediator, and the Holy Spirit guiding your decisions. *"Blessed is the man that heareth me, watching daily at my gates, waiting at the posts of my doors"* (Proverbs 8:34).

How do you hear from God?

You stay close to His gates.

You stay close to His posts.

And then, when the gates are opened through your prayer, you walk right on in.

You stay in the presence of God through the development of prayer in your life. As you develop in your prayer life, your mind is enlightened through renewal. Your understanding of the power of Jesus' Word becomes even greater.

Let'Em Get Mad!

When you begin to flow in your prayer life that way, sometimes people get mad. Let 'em! They were probably already mad to start with and just want to use you as an excuse to keep on being sour.

Really, it's more about pride than anything else. If you don't get sick anymore, they get mad because of it! If you aren't financially broke anymore, they get mad about it! You can see it in their faces. They flinch when you say something good that's going on for you. Do you ever wonder why? Because they're prideful and don't want you to have something they don't have! They want what you've got—they're just not willing to go out and get it through prayer, faith, and patience.

What they're really thinking is, *Just who do you think you are?* You begin to irritate people with your success through prayer. Why? Because they think, *Well, I have been serving God for forty-seven years, and I ain't never had that happen to me.* The amount of time you're a Christian has nothing to do with your capacity to receive from God. Receiving is about faith and knowledge. Faith to believe it can and will be done! Knowledge to know what to do!

People may actually get irritated when you assert your authority as a believer and go boldly to the throne. It's a crying shame! All they have to do is get to God's gate, get to God's door, walk inside the place, and talk to their Father! God will honor His Word to anyone, no matter who they are or how long they've been calling Him Father.

Hearing Brings Responsibility

Hearing from God brings a responsibility to continue the work of Jesus on the earth, which is to lead people to God. When you get born again, God gives you the same vision He gave Jesus—the ministry of reconciliation.

That means we need to reconcile with our brothers and sisters. If you see a brother fall, pick him up. Don't stomp on him. Don't beat him in the head. Don't talk about him behind his back and rail judgment on him. Pick him up and say, "I am going to help you, man. I am going to walk with you. I am going to believe with you."

People make mistakes in life. When you see someone make a mistake, realize that there is something called forgiveness. There's something called love. There is something called grace, mercy, and the most beautiful thing God has to offer—redemption.

You don't have to agree with the sin of the person. You don't have to like what they did. But you can love them despite all their mistakes. That is the vision of Jesus, the ministry of reconciliation.

There's Nothing Wrong with Being an Imitator

When God speaks to me, I have a responsibility not only to Him but also to the vision that God, the Father, gave Jesus. I must continue the work. I must be an imitator of Jesus Christ. The Bible said I've got to in Ephesians 5:1 NIV: *"Be imitators of God, therefore, as dearly loved children."* I don't care what anybody says. If God said that, you've got to do it.

"But I don't feel like it."

It doesn't matter how you feel; it's a fact of being saved! I don't know how many times I've looked across a congregation and said, "Some of you ladies get up in the morning and you don't feel married—but sweetheart, you are!"

There are a lot of times that you don't feel like going to work but you crucify that feeling and go. Why? Because you know it's a requirement and your feelings about it don't matter. You chose the job; so you choose to get up and go to work, even on days that you don't feel like it. Your present feeling doesn't move you. You're moved by your decision.

That's what being a Christian is about too. Sometimes you just don't feel saved. You don't feel like being nice. You don't feel like helping someone out. You don't feel like keeping up Jesus' ministry of reconciliation. You think, *Forget about that idiot! I've got other stuff to do. I ain't got time to mess with him.*

Hey, I understand! I feel the same way too sometimes. We've got to do our best to live right before God, and part of that "living right" is reaching out to other people. Christianity isn't an exclusive lifestyle. It's an inclusive lifestyle—in other words, it should include everybody!

Nobody is left out with Jesus. His ministry is fulfilled when all of us do our part, reaching out to the world wherever we may be. That's how people get saved and touched by God. It's not just the preachers who can do it all. It's everyone, working together to live right and reach out that keeps Jesus' ministry going strong.

"But God, It's 3:00 A.M.!"

Hearing God's voice also brings responsibility to do the individual things He tells you to do. When you start talking to God, you make a commitment to act on what He says to you. That's part of being a doer and not just a hearer.

When God talks to me, He almost always has something for me to do. He isn't a lazy God. He's a God of action. Sometimes, He will wake me up in the middle of the night to talk. I remember one time I was at a hotel, and He woke me up at three o'clock in the morning.

I said, "God, it's three o'clock in the morning!"

"I know," He said, "I created the time. Get up, Jesse."

"What for?"

"I want you to talk to Me."

"But God, it's 3:00 A.M."

"Isn't it nice?" He said, "The television is off."

Whoa! So I got up. But do you know what I did? Out of habit, I got up and went directly towards the television in the hotel room! I didn't even realize I was going there! God spoke to my spirit, "Get your hand off the knob, Jesse. Now, talk to Me."

"God, I am sleepy. I am tired."

He said, "Well, I am going to refresh you."

So I started praying, and my hotel room got really hot. I walked over to the door and opened it up, and cool air blew in. I shouted, "Praise God!" And some guy was walking on the path right outside my room. When he heard me, he jumped and said, "Oh, mister!"

I said, "Did I scare you?"

He said, "Definitely!"

"I am so sorry!"

"That's alright," he said and then looked at me kind of funny. I'd just praised God with a shout at three in the morning, just as he was passing in front of my room. I guess it seemed pretty strange to him!

So I closed the door and went back inside and prayed for the man. I said, "Lord, send the Holy Ghost to him!" And do you know what I heard? I heard the man take off running! He started running down the path! I started laughing and praying, and soon I was really refreshed, just like God had told me I would be.

A Drunk at My Door

Another time, I was preaching a revival and I was staying in a hotel, when all of a sudden, I heard a big, loud thump at my door that sounded like *du-doom!*

I thought, *What is that?* I went to my door, opened it up, and this drunk guy was on the ground right outside my door groaning, "Arrrrrhhhhhh."

I looked down at him and I said, "You need Jesus."

"I am drunk," he slurred and then looked up at me, "and, good God, I got a Jesus freak right here in front of me."

He rolled onto his knees and started to crawl off, drunk out of his mind. His drunk wife was coming down the walkway after him, griping and complaining at him. The drunk man looked back at me and said, "Can you kill her for me?"

I looked at her. She was drunk and storming after him, just eating his head off with all her fussing.

I looked at her coming towards me and said, "Why don't you pray for him?"

She just looked at me with this shocked look, like prayer was the last thing from her drunken mind and kept on walking after her husband.

Anytime you bring God into a situation like that, it shocks people, but especially with drunks! I didn't lead either of them to the Lord that night. Obviously, they weren't in the mood to receive! But it's funny that the man knew a "Jesus freak" when he saw one. Somebody in his life had probably been witnessing to him, and there I was watering their seed on a hotel sidewalk!

Praying in Public

Many times people have walked up to me in public and asked, "Would you pray for me, Brother Jesse?"

Sometimes I immediately say, "Bow your head."

And they'll say, "But not right here, Brother Jesse."

We could be in a grocery store or a restaurant. But I've found out that it is really rare for someone to disrespect the presence of God. Even in a public place, unbelievers will be quiet when the presence of God becomes noticeable. I've even seen them bow their heads before in reverence!

Once I was in a grocery at the express line and a lady in line asked me to pray for her. So I said, "Bow your head."

"Well, not here, Brother Jesse. Not here," she whispered looking around, and she motioned to me that there were others around.

So I looked up and down the line and said, "Everybody, bow your heads." And they all did. They said, "Yeah, OK." I prayed for the woman right there in the line, and no one was offended by the simple prayer. They didn't disrespect it one bit and even agreed to bow their heads. It goes to show you that even sinners will respect the presence of God.

Sometimes the only place you have to pray with someone is in public. If so, don't worry about it, just do it. If others are around and you're worried about what they'll think, ask yourself if you're more worried about what they think than the prayer. What's more important? And if the prayer wins out, all you have to do is be courteous to those around you and say, "Excuse me, but I'm going to pray for this person because they've got a real need."

You don't have to be afraid of unbelievers and what they might think. It's what God thinks that matters. Needs are too great to be stifled by worry over what others may think. Prayers are too important to be stifled by that.

Praying in the Sauna

Sometimes I pray in front of unbelievers, and I don't even realize I'm doing it! A while back I was taking a sauna bath after I exercised, and there were a few men in there. I said, "Whoa, it is hot," and because I'd been praying while I was exercising I said, "Praise the Lord, thank You, Jesus." It just came out of my mouth.

If you want to clear a space quick, just say the name of Jesus. Anybody who's not interested in hearing it will leave pretty fast! That sauna was empty in a few seconds flat. I figure that if they can cuss, then I can pray. I was never embarrassed to cuss in public when I was a heathen. Why should I be embarrassed to pray in public now that I'm saved?

But there is a difference. Jesus is being lifted up. And demons flee when they hear His name. Unless a person is ready to receive Jesus or is contemplating it, their mind will tell them, "Get out! Get out! Get out!"

Do you ever wonder why that fear comes on some people when you say the name of Jesus? Because Jesus' name is powerful, that's why! Angels bow to it and demons tremble at the sound of that name. If it's coming across the lips of a person who has actual faith in that name, watch out! The room will clear out.

People who are running from God will run from the name of Jesus. Those who are searching for God won't immediately go. They may stay and talk, maybe even ask a few questions. Some might not receive what you say, but they'll listen if they're searching. They might not even know they're searching.

You may be reading this book right now, and you don't know why you even picked it up and began reading it. If that is you, some of the stuff in this book may sound as foreign as another language and you might not believe much of it, but if you're still reading it, chances are you're searching for something. That something is God, and all of us need Him in our lives.

I hope you reach out to Him and talk to Him. If you don't open up to one other person on this earth, open up to God. He's really a good Father. He loves you, no matter who you are or where you've been, and He wants to have a real relationship with you.

CHAPTER 24

The Cost of Hearing God's Voice

In Jesus' earthly ministry, He had a couple of women who really loved Him and what He taught. They were Mary and Martha, and they had a brother named Lazarus. You've probably heard the story before, but I want to share some points with you that I think will help you out.

Lazarus knew Jesus personally. He and his two sisters ate with Jesus and talked with Jesus—Jesus even slept over at the family's house from time to time when He was in town.

So Lazarus gets sick and his sisters try and get in touch with Jesus. But Jesus is doing a meeting out of town and can't get to their house right away.

Mary sends a message to Jesus that says, "Look Jesus, if You don't get down here soon, my brother is going to die. We're working against the clock down here. The man is sick. He's grievously tormented. He's going to die!"

The woman was burying him with her words by being so fearful and speaking death over him. Almost every time He prayed and someone got healed, Jesus would say something like, "Your faith has made you whole." Martha and Mary just didn't understand the power of belief when it came to healing yet.

Now, the devil messed up when he tried to take Lazarus' life because this man was Jesus' friend, and besides, God doesn't believe in premature death.

If you will do a study in the Bible, you'll find out that everybody Jesus raised from the dead was young. You don't read about Him raising ninety-year-old women. You read about Him raising up young people. That's because their time isn't up yet, and the devil has just succeeded at stealing their life from them. It's not God's will for people to die young, but the devil will do everything he can to "steal, kill and destroy" God's people. Psalm 91:16 says, *"With long life will I satisfy him, and shew him my salvation."* Long life is God's plan. But the devil took a shot at Lazarus and won—for a couple of days anyway.

Jesus heard about Lazarus' death, but it didn't make a difference to Him how dead Lazarus was. One day, two days, three days, or four—dead is dead. In Jewish tradition, the person wasn't considered really dead until three days. So it's fitting that Jesus chose the fourth day to see about Lazarus.

Now, Lazarus' dead body was in the grave. But the combination of his soul and spirit, which is the real Lazarus, was not entombed in that grave. Yet he wasn't in Heaven either. Heaven is for those who receive Jesus as Lord. Jesus hadn't gone to the cross yet, so where is Lazarus? In Paradise. He's in a place that existed for all those who loved God and died before Jesus went to the cross—in Paradise, a place the Bible also calls Abraham's bosom. This is where all the Old Testament men and women of God went after death.

So Lazarus is hanging out with people like Abraham, Isaac, and Jacob. The cares of this physical world are gone from his mind. He is at peace, in bliss and just enjoying himself in Paradise. But his family is grieving, and there is a miracle about to happen that is going to jerk this boy right out of Paradise!

John 11:17-43 tells the details of the story:

"Then when Jesus came, he found that he had lain in the grave four days already. Now Bethany was nigh unto Jerusalem, about fifteen furlongs off: And many of the Jews came to Martha and Mary, to comfort them concerning their brother. Then Martha, as soon as she heard that Jesus was coming, went and met him: but Mary sat still in the house.

"Then said Martha unto Jesus, Lord, if thou hadst been here, my brother had not died. But I know, that even now, whatsoever thou wilt ask of God, God will give it thee.

"Jesus saith unto her, Thy brother shall rise again.

"Martha saith unto him, I know that he shall rise again in the resurrection at the last day.

"Jesus said unto her, I am the resurrection, and the life: he that believeth in me, though he were dead, yet shall he live: And whosoever liveth and believeth in me shall never die. Believest thou this?

"She saith unto him, Yea, Lord: I believe that thou art the Christ, the Son of God, which should come into the world. And when she had so said, she went her way, and called Mary her sister secretly, saying, The Master is come, and calleth for thee.

"As soon as she heard that, she arose quickly, and came unto him. Now Jesus was not yet come into the town, but was

*in that place where Martha met him. The Jews then which
were with her in the house, and comforted her, when they saw
Mary, that she rose up hastily and went out, followed her,
saying, She goeth unto the grave to weep there.*

"*Then when Mary was come where Jesus was, and
saw him, she fell down at his feet, saying unto him, Lord, if
thou hadst been here, my brother had not died. When Jesus
therefore saw her weeping, and the Jews also weeping which
came with her, he groaned in the spirit, and was troubled, And
said, Where have ye laid him? They said unto him, Lord, come
and see.*

"*Jesus wept.*

"*Then said the Jews, Behold how he loved him!*

"*And some of them said, Could not this man, which
opened the eyes of the blind, have caused that even this man
should not have died?*

"*Jesus therefore again groaning in himself cometh to the
grave. It was a cave, and a stone lay upon it. Jesus said, Take
ye away the stone. Martha, the sister of him that was dead,
saith unto him, Lord, by this time he stinketh: for he hath been
dead four days.*

"*Jesus saith unto her, Said I not unto thee, that, if thou
wouldest believe, thou shouldest see the glory of God? Then
they took away the stone from the place where the dead was
laid.*

"*And Jesus lifted up his eyes, and said, Father, I thank
thee that thou hast heard me. And I knew that thou hearest*

*Me always: but because of the people which stand by I said it, that they may believe that thou hast sent Me. And when he thus had spoken, he cried with a loud voice, **Lazarus, come forth.***"

The Unwelcome Command

At this moment, Lazarus is in Paradise, and from that place, he hears a voice—Jesus' voice.

"Lazarus! Come forth!"

Lazarus turns to see where the voice is coming from. He may have been in conversation with Abraham, but suddenly that voice of the Lord comes through air—"Lazarus...." Listening and realizing what the call meant, Lazarus may have thought to himself, *But I don't want to go back, Lord.*

That is typically what people say who have returned from the afterlife. It's a freedom and peace they don't want to leave, even when they go earlier than they should. Jesus was groaning in His spirit right before this. Do you ever wonder why? Of course we know He was saddened because He wept. He knew His friend had died young, and He watched as the family was in such grief and even blaming Him that if He'd only been there, it wouldn't have happened.

But the groaning could have also been because He knew that both sides were pulling on Him. Mary and Martha were in despair, wanting their brother back. Lazarus was free and happy where he was, even if he wasn't supposed to be there yet. But no matter where you are, when the Boss talks, you listen.

The voice of the Son of God was speaking.

"Lazarus, come forth."

And do you know what happened? Lazarus came forth!

The power of Jesus' command sucked young Lazarus out of Paradise and pushed his spirit-soul back into his mortal flesh. The power of Jesus' simple words put him back on earth and in the grave, bound with burial clothes and suddenly struggling to get loose.

I'm back, Lazarus probably thought to himself. *I am alive!*

"And he that was dead came forth, bound hand and foot with graveclothes: and his face was bound about with a napkin. Jesus saith unto them, Loose him, and let him go" (v. 44).

Lazarus was in Paradise just enjoying himself, but it wasn't God's plan for him to stay there. He was too young.

We All Have an Appointed Time

If you were to equate death with punctuation, you could say that death is not the end of a sentence. It's not a period; it's just a comma. It's like a pause in the flow of the sentence. After the pause, you still keep reading.

Since Jesus came to the earth, when we die we go on and live in another place—Heaven or Hell. I like to say that there will be no unbelievers after death! Everybody will believe whether they want to or not!

We all have an appointed time to die, and after this comes the judgment of the God according to Hebrews 9:27. Sometimes the devil steals a life before its appointed time, but we all have a time to die, and it's important that we do what we can to keep the appointment—and don't show up earlier than we should!

Sometimes in life people actually want to go earlier. Did you know that Paul the Apostle was trying to die for years before he was supposed to? He talked to God about it, begging Him to get him out of here. But he ended up saying that for your sake, it was better for him to stay. He knew the Lord had a destiny for him to fulfill, even though he wanted to go home to Heaven. God called Paul to the Gentiles, and He didn't want him leaving earth until that foundation of truth was laid plain for the Gentile people.

That's why when Paul was on death row, he didn't bawl and squall about dying. Instead Paul said, and I'll paraphrase, "Give me a piece of paper. I am going to write down one more revelation before I go home to be with God."

He was still taking care of his body because he said, "Give me a coat."

He was still taking care of his mind because he said, "Give me some books."

He was taking care of his destiny by saying, "But give me the parchments. Let me tell you more about what God has said."

He understood that before his appointment with death, he had to fulfill his destiny. But Paul wanted to die and go on to Heaven. It cost him to stick around, but the rewards went far beyond the cost. Today we have much of the New Testament because of the apostle Paul!

When it comes to the death of Lazarus, there was a cost involved in hearing God's voice too. Lazarus was hanging out in Paradise, but Jesus knew that he had gone too early. He wasn't where he should be. Jesus knew that Lazarus should have still been on earth with his sisters. It wasn't his time to die yet, but that terrible sickness had taken him early.

But it cost Lazarus to hear and obey God's voice.

It put off his time in Paradise for quite a few more years.

The Cost of Obeying His Voice

As a minister, I travel a great deal. It is what God has called me to do. He spoke to me, called me to this office of the evangelist, and commissioned me to *"Go ye into all the world, and preach the gospel to every creature"* (Mark 16:15).

That's not easy all the time. Sometimes I don't want to leave home. I've got a beautiful wife. Sometimes I don't want to leave. I look at her sometimes and think, *God, I have been on the road for so long. I don't want to go anymore.* But He has called me with His voice to "Go ye!"

As an evangelist, I'm grateful and blessed to have more invitations than I can fill. But sometimes I just want to stay home, when God has told me to go. There is a pull between wanting what I want and what God wants. It's what all of us sometimes encounter when God has spoken to us, told us what to do, but it goes against our own plans. It's the unwelcome voice of God at work.

Hearing the voice of Jesus has cost me some of my family time. Not all, but a lot. Yet I know I am doing what God wants me to do. And people are being led to Jesus through my ministry by the thousands. My rewards in Heaven will be great, and He is even rewarding me on earth.

Rewards for Following His Voice

As a minister of the Gospel, I stand on His Scripture in Mark 10:29,30: *"And Jesus answered and said, Verily I say unto you, There is no man that hath left house, or brethren, or sisters, or father, or mother, or wife, or children, or lands, for my sake, and the gospel's, But he shall receive an hundredfold now in this time, houses, and brethren, and sisters, and mothers, and children, and lands, with persecutions; and in the world to come eternal life."*

Those who choose to follow the voice of God in ministry and forsake all are rewarded in this life and in the next. Now, it does say those rewards come with persecution in this life, but they're worth it. What doesn't come with persecution on this earth? Not much! The devil is out there trying to steal, kill, and destroy all the time. But God is here all the time too. And I've read the end of the Book. We win! So I say, "Take your best shot, devil. I've got God on my side, and I'm winning!"

There's No Sense Begging

Sometimes when I'm preaching on the road, I hear people praying and it's as if they are asking the devil to give them back what he's stolen. I wonder why some people think that they have to beg the devil to give back the stuff he stole from them. It's like they're pleading with him to give it up.

I want to shout, "The devil doesn't listen to reason! He isn't giving up anybody's stuff without a fight. It's called the good fight of faith."

Faith and authority is what the devil responds to. Sometimes I'm praying about what the devil has stolen from me and I say, "Give me that, devil!" And he says, "No!" and fights me tooth and nail. I have to use the Scriptures, my sword, to get back my stuff. I have to use my faith and my God-given authority as His kid!

Being in tune with God's Holy Spirit really helps you to feel confident. Jesus was confident, so we should follow His example in life. He wasn't a wimp. He didn't play games with the devil. He rebuked the devil, cast the devil out, and resisted the devil. Jesus was powerful. He prayed a lot. He'd go in the wilderness and just be alone with His Father.

Jesus was so in tune with His Father that His perception of spiritual things was off the charts! It was like He had an antenna pointed towards His Dad's throne. There would be thousands of people waiting to be healed, and God would send a thought to Jesus, *Go to the mountain and pray.* Jesus would leave the crowd on the beach, saying "I'll be back later. I must talk to My Father."

He didn't let people's opinion of what He should do rule His life. He did what God told Him do. He used His faith as a channel for the power of God, and He accomplished amazing miracles that inspire us today.

Jesus was a man of power!

CHAPTER 25

The Power in His Voice

Evangelism is God's vision for the earth. He gave it to Jesus, and Jesus has given it to you and to me. Jesus gave life to a dead man when He raised Lazarus from the dead. And He did it with His voice.

There is power in the voice of God. It's not vocal power; it's spiritual power, and it's in us too. Now, I've never had the faith to do what Jesus did in this instance, to call a dead man back from the afterlife. But I may get there one day! You don't hear about raising the dead too much today, I think it's because we don't have much faith for it today, and I also believe it's because when believers die today, they go to Heaven and are in the very presence of God. It's hard to leave somewhere like that. It's far better than mere Paradise. When you're looking at the face of God, this place looks like a pit!

There is amazing power in the voice of God though. And there is power in us because the Word we speak is His Word. When we speak God's Words and minister His saving love, it can reach people's hearts and pull them out of a pit of darkness. Like Lazarus, it can jerk them out of where they are, in the pit of sin and depression, and cause them to rise up! To rise up and walk to the altar and say, "I want to see this

Jesus. I want to make Him my Lord." That's people responding to the power of the Word of God.

Come Unto Me...

Jesus is calling everyone to Him. He doesn't want one person to miss out on knowing God as their friend and Father. He doesn't want His blood to miss one person. He wants to use His sacrifice to wash away everyone's sin so that all can freely communicate with His Holy Spirit.

There is great power of sharing Jesus with others. The problems of the world beat people up and they need help. Jesus is here. He's not absent. He's available. His very name means "God with us," and we can share that with people we meet. We can all do the work of an evangelist simply by telling others what we know.

We don't have to know everything to share the message of Jesus with others. The life of a Christian is a journey in learning more about God, His Word, and how to apply it to our daily lives. Nobody arrives at perfection until they meet their Maker face to face in Heaven! Until then, we live out each day visiting with God, learning more about Him through His Word, applying what we learn, using the gifts He's given, and sharing what we know with other people.

And it's a good life.

In Matthew 11:28 Jesus said, *"Come unto me, all ye that labour and are heavy laden, and I will give you rest."* Notice it doesn't say, "Come unto me all those who want lots of trouble." It's not a warning of the dire situations of life! It's simply a command to come and to find some peace in knowing Jesus. That Scripture is for everyone. It's for those who don't know God and need peace. It's for those who do know God and have allowed this world's problems to destroy their hope, self-esteem, and optimism for a better future.

Jesus never said, "Come unto Me, and I will give you cancer." Or,-"Come unto Me, and I'll give you poverty." He promised to give you *rest.*

Coming to Jesus doesn't mean you get a load of more problems. It means you get more solutions. It's not a heavy load you have to carry. It's an easy package that simply makes life livable—and even fun! I think it is great knowing God. Who wouldn't want to communicate with their Maker?

Jesus promises, *"Take my yoke upon you, and learn of me; for I am meek and lowly in heart: and ye shall find rest unto your souls. For my yoke is easy, and my burden is light"* (Matthew 11:29,30).

I don't know what you may be carrying around with you today. But whatever it is, just remember this: If it's heavy, it's not from God! And it's not meant for you. Knowing Jesus is a good way to live. Sometimes our families, churches, and jobs put heavy burdens on us, but Jesus never does.

His yoke is easy.

His burden is light.

He wants you to know that His Holy Spirit is with you every step of the way. When Jesus was talking to His disciples before He went to the cross, He made them a promise that is still alive today.

He promised that when He went to Heaven, He was going to prepare a place for us. And not just any place—a mansion! What is a mansion by Heaven's standards? It is definitely better than anything we can build on earth!

Jesus was a carpenter when He walked this earth. He's still building today! He's the Master Carpenter Who is at work in Heaven preparing for the day you come home. Now, if He's that concerned with your heavenly home, don't you think He cares about your earthly-home? Don't you think He cares about your family? Your friends? Your job? Your relationships? Your needs and the desires of your heart?

When I was a kid growing up in church, I never heard that God was really interested in my daily life. Now that I know Him and know what His Word says, I know that He is definitely interested in my daily life!

Jesus went to the cross to die for me. He cared about my soul, but He cared about so much more than that. Life is a precious and holy thing. Jesus said in John 10:10 that He came to give us life, and to give it to us in abundance.

We begin the abundant life when we open our hearts to God, open our minds to His Word, and present our bodies as living sacrifices to Him. God knows we can't do it on our own! He knows we're human and make mistakes. But He loves us with the love of a Father—a good Father Who wants the very best for His kids.

As I end this book, I want you to know that no matter where you go or what you do in life, the voice and direction of God is available to you. God speaks in many ways: through that still, small voice in your heart; through the Scriptures; through His audible voice; and through the gifts of the Holy Spirit. He speaks through dreams, visions, and many odd, odd ways too!

Your Father is looking for ways to talk to you. He loves you. He cares about you and wants you to have joy in your heart, to enjoy the blessings of a full, long life, and to be at peace knowing that He is always there for you.

Never make the mistake of thinking you're alone because you're not. Never make the mistake of thinking that nobody understands you because God knows you better than you even know yourself! You never have to feel alone or misunderstood in this crazy world because your Father will never abandon you, and He always understands just what you're trying to say!

No matter what, you can be confident that you've got a God you can talk to. Best of all, God is willing to talk *back* to you! So start up a conversation with Him today. Keep your heart open, let your doubts fall by the wayside, and soon you'll discover just how wonderful it is to be in communion with God!

Prayer of Salvation

A born-again, committed relationship with God is the key to the victorious life. Jesus, the Son of God, laid down His life and rose again so that we could spend eternity with Him in Heaven and experience His absolute best on earth. The Bible says, *"For God so loved the world, that he gave his only begotten Son, that whosoever believeth in him should not perish, but have everlasting life"* (John 3:16).

It is the will of God that everyone receive eternal salvation. The way to receive this salvation is to call upon the name of Jesus and confess Him as your Lord. The Bible says, *"That if thou shalt confess with thy mouth the Lord Jesus, and shalt believe in thine heart that God hath raised him from the dead, thou shalt be saved. For whosoever shall call upon the name of the Lord shall be saved"* (Romans 10:9-10,13).

Jesus has given salvation, healing, and countless benefits to all who call upon His name. These benefits can be yours if you receive Him into your heart by praying this prayer:

Heavenly Father, I come to You admitting that I am a sinner. Right now, I choose to turn away from sin, and I ask You to cleanse me of all unrighteousness. I believe that Your Son, Jesus, died on the cross to take away my sins. I also believe that He rose again from the dead so that I may be justified and made righteous through faith in Him. I call upon the name of Jesus Christ to be the Savior and Lord of my life. Jesus, I choose to follow You, and I ask that You fill me with the power of the Holy Spirit. I declare that right now, I am a born-again child of God. I am free from sin and full of the righteousness of God. I am saved in Jesus' name, Amen.

If you have prayed this prayer to receive Jesus Christ as your Savior, or if this book has changed your life, we would like to hear from you. Please write us at:

Jesse Duplantis Ministries
PO Box 1089
Destrehan, LA 70047
985.764.2000
www.jdm.org

About the Author

Jesse Duplantis is what some would call a true evangelist. Supernaturally saved and delivered from a life of addiction in 1974 and called by God to the office of the evangelist in 1978, he founded Jesse Duplantis Ministries with one mission in his mind and one vision in his heart—global evangelism, whatever the cost. And throughout his many years of evangelistic ministry, he has sought to do just that.

With a television ministry that spans the globe, ministry offices in America, the United Kingdom, and Australia, and a preaching itinerary that has taken him to over 1,000 different churches to date, Jesse is still fulfilling his original call to evangelism with gusto! His commitment to Christ, long-standing integrity in ministry, and infectious, joyful nature have made him one of the most loved and respected ministers of the gospel today. Oral Roberts Ministries recognized his achievements in the field of evangelism by awarding him an honorary doctorate of divinity in 1999.

A Cajun from Southern Louisiana, Jesse makes the Bible easy to understand by preaching its truths in our everyday vernacular and spicing his messages with humor. Often called the "Apostle of Joy" because of hilarious illustrations, Jesse's anointed preaching and down-to-earth style have helped to open the door for countless numbers of people to receive Jesus as their Lord and Savior. Jesse has proven through his own life that no matter who you are or where you come from, God can change your heart, develop your character through His Word, and help you find and complete your divine destiny.

To contact Jesse Duplantis Ministries,
write or call:

Jesse Duplantis Ministries
PO Box 1089
Destrehan, Louisiana 70047
985.764.2000
www.jdm.org

Please include your prayer requests, praise reports
and comments when you write.

Other Books by Jesse Duplantis

The Big 12

LIVING AT THE TOP

For By IT...FAITH

DISTORTION: The Vanity of Genetically Altered Christianity

Breaking The Power of Natural Law

What in Hell Do You Want?

Jambalaya for the Soul

God Is Not Enough, He's Too Much!

Heaven—Close Encounters of the God Kind
Also available in Spanish

Why Isn't My Giving Working? The Four Types of Giving

The Ministry of Cheerfulness

The Sovereignty of God

Running Toward Your Giant

Don't Be Affected by the World's Message

Keep Your Foot on the Devil's Neck

Leave It in the Hands of a Specialist

One More Night With the Frogs

The Battle of Life

Understanding Salvation
Also available in Spanish

Available at your local bookstore.